Derby
Memories

The publishers would like to thank the following companies for their

Main Sponsor
Mertrux Limited

Derbyshire Fire and Rescue Service

Garrandale Group

MHA Care Group

Midlands Co-operative Society Limited

Moody & Woolley

Parry Group

Picture The Past

Smith of Derby

Thorntons Plc

University of Derby

G Walthall & Son Limited

W W Winter Limited

First published in Great Britain by True North Books Limited
England HX3 6AE
01422 344344

ISBN 1 903204 96 8

Text, design and origination by True North Books
Printed and bound by The Amadeus Press

Derby Memories

A happy group in Roe Street (now Roe Walk) who chose all manner of costumes to celebrate the Queen's Coronation in 1953

CONTENTS

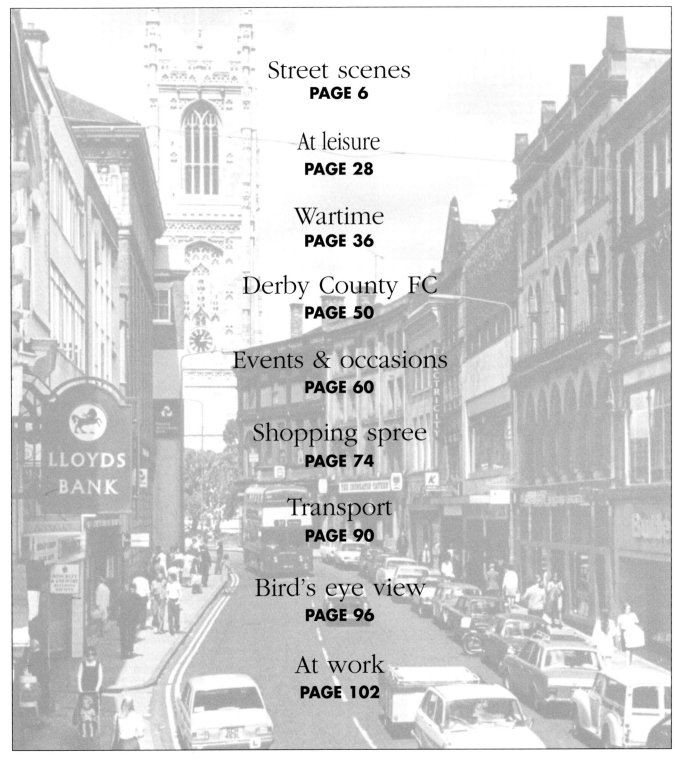

INTRODUCTION

Derby is the UK's most central city on the edge of the Peak District National park. It is famous for setting in motion Britain's Industrial Revolution with some of the country's first factories and spinning mills. It is equally famous for its later factories of Rolls Royce and Royal Crown Derby, and for railway engineering. In prehistoric times Derby was the lowest place where the Derwent could be forded. There were stone circles at Arbor Low. Gold bracelets, bronze daggers and pottery have been found nearby, dating back to nearly 2000 BC. In the 9th century AD the town of Derby was founded by the Danes as Deoraby. 'Der' is a corruption of 'deer' and 'by' is simply the Norse for 'village'.

Derby grew under the Normans. Early Royal Charters were granted in 1154-56 and 1204. All Saints Church (a cathedral from 1927) with its tower, 210 feet high, was built in 1509-27.

Silk throwing, or spinning by machine, was introduced into the town from Italy in 1719. Many people in Derby were employed in the manufacture of silk hosiery, lace and cotton. The manufacture of porcelain in the locality began in 1750. After a visit by George III in 1773, the town was granted a patent to mark its china with a crown, and the local product was to be forever known as Crown Derby. This became Royal Crown Derby with the blessing of Queen Victoria in 1890. A canal network helped Derby's early factories. In the 19th century the city became a major railway centre. Rail and aircraft engineering would become important industries. Whilst the links with earlier days are important, it is however on more recent times that we will be concentrating. Opening the first page of this book you are embarking on a journey that will take you back over the decades of the last century.

Each photograph is enhanced by carefully researched captions. Both wry and informative, the text takes the reader beyond the image to times that have gone forever. This book is not however meant to be a dry historical tome, but one that unleashes waves of nostalgia. Join with the photographer and caption-writer to take a stroll along memory lane that take us from the elegance of Edwardians promenading along London Road to the deregulated buses whizzing around the city centre today. In between we can recall the times when Rudolf Valentino was the screen heartthrob and Lassie came home. Then there was the poverty of the depression years. Add to that the losses in two world wars. But there were many happier times. Recall the jolly days when we played tig in the park; the days before mobile phones, computers and video games; times when television was still a miracle, even if its pictures were only in black and white. You are about to enter a world where the washing machine was a luxury, and donkey stoning the front step was still a work of art. This book will help you remember the taste of ginger beer and dandelion and burdock. Here, wind-up record players still scratch out melodies recorded on 78s as Bobby-soxers swoon to the sounds of Sinatra, Johnny Ray and Guy Mitchell: others will recall the excitement of buying the new 45s on which they listened to Elvis, the Beatles and the Rolling Stones on their ultra-modern Dansette record players. So turn off that digital satellite TV and settle back in your favourite chair. It is time to think of trams and trolley buses, coal fires and pounds shillings and pence. Within the pages of this book the reader will be able to return to those days when our monarchs were revered and our newsreels were full of British achievement. Derby has much to be proud of and a number of its best known and longest established firms have allowed us to access their internal archives. This has enabled us to recount the history of these companies from humble beginnings, in most cases, to leading positions in their chosen area of expertise. These organisations have tremendous social, as well as commercial significance, as between them they represent the places of employment for many thousands of Derby people. We are very grateful to the directors of these businesses for their co-operation and valuable support. Let the nostalgia begin!

TEXT	ROY GREENWOOD, STEVE AINSWORTH
PHOTOGRAPH COMPILATION	TONY LAX
DESIGNER	SEAMUS MOLLOY
BUSINESS DEVELOPMENT EDITOR	PETER PREST

STREET SCENES

S t Peter's Street is a busy shopping street in the city and has long been so as this picture taken around 1930 clearly demonstrates. In fact if you follow a line down St Peter's Street it will take in the path of the ancient north–south trackway that existed long before Derby itself came into existence. And if you consider today's traffic to be bad, it was the same problem for drivers along this city street in the 1930s. It was a case of buses, bicycles and many private cars. Fortunately there were fewer heavy goods vehicles, but at least one made it along St Peter's Street in this picture. The tram lines diverge at this point in the picture, looking from The Spot. There are as many shops, banks and businesses along today's St Peter's Street as there were when this picture was taken. One particular one is Edwards' glass and china shop on the left in this picture One notable spot in St Peter's Street is Babington Buildings, which houses Waterstone's. There, high above your head, you will see a carving of two baboons either side of a barrel or tun, giving "baboon-tun" or Babington. Babington Buildings was built to house the Derby branch of the Public Benefit Boot and Shoe Company in 1898, with offices for rent on the upper floors. The house on the site, pulled down in 1897, was latterly called Babington House. It was a Jacobean mansion of splendid appearance and, at the time, its demolition was much regretted by certain sections of Derby society.

Above and below: These two pictures of the Guildhall were taken 15 years apart, but both show one of the features which dominated Derby city centre for decades – trolley bus wires. The upright photograph was taken in 1935 and shows the criss-cross of the wires, while the panoramic view taken around 1950 gives a much more artistic feel to them. After the previous building was gutted by fire in 1841, the current Guildhall was completely rebuilt a year later by Henry Duesbury, grandson of the founder of the Derby China Factory. Derby's Guildhall is now a theatre and is one of the mainstays of entertainment in the city. Situated on Market Place, it puts on a variety of plays, concerts and shows throughout the year, often by local theatrical groups. The Guildhall is also used as a club centre and a studio for local artists to exhibit their work. Opposite Derby's Guildhall there is a permanent "installation sculpture" that consists of a semi circular waterfall. Beneath the Guildhall is a labyrinth of tunnels and catacombs. One of the tunnels used to link the old police station (lock-up) – the building to the left of the Guildhall - in Lock-Up Yard to the Assize Courts, which were at that time in the Guildhall. Many prisoners have trudged along those dark, dank tunnels from the lock-up to the courts, where they were sentenced, and then trudged back into the lock-up to be then taken away to be executed, transported, or imprisoned. Many people say they have heard ghostly footsteps in the tunnels.

Below: This familiar and much-photographed Derby street is well known to local folk. But the era featured is less familiar, for it reflects an age when it was less dangerous to loiter in the middle of a retail street among cars and buses which pose such a danger in modern times. Thankfully the introduction of pedestrian precincts has added to the safety of town centre shoppers in shopping centres throughout the country. The photographer was looking towards Market Head when he released the shutter for this picture. In the distance the distinctive light coloured outline of Barlow Taylor and Company's store can be seen. Of course, the building later found fame (and probably fortune) as the imposing public face of the Derby Building Society. The tudor-styled property on the right of the street has always created interest in Derby. It was best remembered as the home of Cox and Malin and the location of their wine importing business which was to display the Guinness is Good For You sign for many decades. Cox and Malin's business stood between two other retail outfits which had achieved national importance. One was H. Samuel's, remembered in Derby as in other locations, for its distinctive exterior clock and reputation for supplying a wide range of good-quality, affordable items of jewellry. It would be interesting to know just how many Derby couples have peered through Samuels' window, prior to making their commitment to each other with symbolic band of gold bought here.

Right: 'The Spot' pictured here in the happy Edwardian days prior the first world war is something of a mystery. Its name is a curiosity, no one seems to know how it came to be called the Spot although there are several theories. The area's origins are lost in the mists of antiquity though from this well known landmark it is possible to look down St Peter's Street and follow the line of the ancient north–south track that existed long before Derby came into existence. A bronze statue of Queen Victoria was sited here in 1906, donated by the famous Derby Engineer Sir Alfred Searle Haslam. King Edward VII unveiled it on the 28th June that year. Some 22 years later the statue was moved to a site in front of the Derby Royal Infirmary. Queen Victoria and her husband Prince Albert, passed through Derby on their way to Chatsworth in 1843. Six years later they were back in Derby again when they and their family stayed at the Midland Hotel. Her Majesty was presented with a loyal address from the Corporation. The Queen paid her only State visit to Derby in 1891 when she laid the

foundation stone of the new Derbyshire Royal Infirmary, and during the course of her visit knighted the Mayor, Alderman Alfred Seale Haslam. Subsequently The Spot would become the site for a well-concealed underground toilet block that because of the City Council's Derby Promenade scheme of the 1990s would become even less conspicuous.

Bottom left: Countless 'household name' shops in Derby have been lost down the years in the name of progress: their memory is now consigned to the 'retail heritage' category of local history. One of the best-remembered shops in St Peter's Street was the Central Educational Co. Ltd. The shop sold books, pictures, artists and drawing materials, craftwork items, fine china, and all manner of giftware under the general heading of what we used to commonly refer to as 'fancy goods'. Informally known as the 'Central Ed', it was a popular shop for youngsters stocking up with materials for each new school term. Throughout the first half of the 20th century the large establishment in St. Peter's Street was a favourite haunt of school children and their parents. Sadly the business moved to smaller premises in St. Peter's Churchyard in the 1960s, before eventually closing down in the early 1990s. Meanwhile

thousands of readers will recall visiting 'Central Ed' to buy new pencil sets, crayons and geometry sets back in the days when log tables and brain power were the way to work out difficult sums rather than calculators. Most children today will think of blotting paper as being as archaic as quill pens and parchment, yet bottles of ink bottles, blotting paper and metal pen nibs were still standard school equipment until the 1960s. A new fountain pen was always on every child's Christmas and birthday list. Many teachers objected to pupils using the new-fangled biros which they said led to poor handwriting.

Below: The 1930s were a time of big changes in Derby city centre with re-development being on everyone's lips. It continued throughout the decade and only paused with the outbreak of the second world war in 1939. Certainly it was still high on the list for discussion in 1938, when this picture was taken. Congestion was the subject of this photograph, with buses, trolley buses, cars vans, lorries and masses of people all trying to make their way along Nottingham Road. This picture was taken by Hurst and Wallis, who were technical photographers for the council's City Engineers Department. It shows the congestion in the "rush hour" of Thursday 1st September, 1938, between 4.30pm and 5.15pm, and was taken to assess traffic flow for potential road re-development.

Below: Repton was the old capital of the Mercian kingdom and the village, just a few miles south west of Derby city centre, is the cradle of Christianity in the Midlands. A monastery was founded here in 653 AD and Christians have worshipped on this site ever since. In the picture is Saint Wystan's church in Repton. It was built around 975 AD and was extensively altered during the 13th to 15th centuries. The Anglo-Saxon crypt under St Wystan's dates back to the 7th century. The crypt is one of the oldest and most important examples of Anglo-Saxon architecture to survive intact. Sir John Betjeman described it as "holy air encased in stone". The church is a prominent landmark and around here there are buildings from the 8th Century to modern times including the old Priory that dates from the 12th and 13th Centuries, but 18th and 19th Century buildings now dominate the scene. The picture dates back to long before the wide-open street shown became one of the main traffic routes through Repton. On the left of the picture is the ancient Market Cross, where four main road meet and which today forms a roundabout at the busy junction. The Cross has medieval origins is the centre of Medieval Repton, where there used to be a market and a summer fair until 1900. There was also an autumn fair for the hiring of domestic servants and farm labour. C.B. Fry, perhaps the best all-round sportsman England ever had, is buried in St. Wystan's Churchyard.

Flooding is no laughing matter as many people found to their cost in England during 2007, but these pictures from 1932 show the problems in Derby city centre during the great flood of 1932. While the floodwater brought misery to most, these kids saw the lighter side of the problem outside Woolworth's in Victoria Street and this lone boatman to opportunity to practise his oarsmanship on the deep water which engulfed Cornmarket. Inhabitants of Derby had in fact seen the worst floods in the city for 50 years in September 1931. But these were surpassed just months later when 36 hours of rain fell around 22nd May 1932. The city centre was submerged as the water came halfway up the windows. The damage was estimated at £400,000 and the Mayor launched a relief fund. The shops were badly hit but soon drew customers back with special "salvage sales". It was heartbreak, however, for many of the poorer people in the Markeaton Brook area who lost everything when the Markeaton Brook culvert which runs through the centre of the city overflowed, being unable to cope with the rising volume of water. A consultant engineer was brought in to find a way of preventing this happening again. His recommendations were similar to those suggested by Herbert Spencer many years earlier. In 1938 the Markeaton Brook relief culvert was finished. It seemed to work because in 1960 over two inches of rain fell in 24 hours, but this time there was no flooding in the city centre.

Right: Here we are looking up St Peter's Street in a shot thought to have been taken not long after the end of the first world war. On the left where the clock is mounted on the wall is where Marks & Spencer's would eventually open. To the right was the Central Educational shop, still remembered by many today. Only a distant tram reminds us that the street was not a pedestrian precinct in those long ago days when motor vehicles were so slow moving and uncommon. Pedestrians could happily walk in the street as freely as they wished, hampered only by the hazard posed by horse droppings. The two ladies in the foreground are still wearing Edwardian dress. This would soon change as the fashions of the 'roaring twenties' arrived in Derby leading to shockingly high hemlines exposing previously hidden calves to public view. One of the curious facts about early

photographs, especially portrait photos, is how misleading they often are in relation to clothing. Naturally folk who knew they were going to be photographed dressed in their best and most fashionable clothes. In their work people often wore very different and very worn clothes that today make them look like inhabitants of an impoverished third world country. Meanwhile here is a world where few folk have even seen an aeroplane let alone flown in one. Electric lighting s a rarity, no public radio station has ever been listened to, and moving pictures are silent and in black and white.

Left: By the early part of the 13th century the Market Place in Derby was known to have been a busy commercial centre with shops and stalls. The first street names appear around this time: Newland Street from around 1190, St James' Lane, now St James' Street, and Sadler Gate are both first mentioned about 1250. Getting on for seven hundred years later and St James Street has evolved to look like this. In this picture taken between the wars St James Street looks peaceful and prosperous. After four years of insanity between 1914 and 1918 the world was at last getting back to normal; prams which had been a relatively rare feature on the streets in the war years were now back in force as a baby boom took place. Hats too are very evident in this picture. Social class was displayed in many ways. After all we need to know our place! Workingmen wore flat caps, middle class men trilbies and the better classes bowlers. In London toffs still wore top hats. In fact however people were increasingly forgetting their place: servants were hard to find as millions of women who had been 'in service' were finding better-paid jobs elsewhere. Many women now had the vote; soon all women over 21 years of age would have the same privilege. In politics the working classes were making their voice heard in the shape of the Labour Party which was gaining increasing strength and would eventually eclipse the Liberals.

Above: On the right hand side of Albert Street, seen from its junction with Victoria Street, there is the former Trent bus station, with its panelled roof and triangular infill. Before it was a bus station it was a fish market, and after it was pulled down in 1986 it was used as a bus park, where on a cold and frosty morning at start up time you couldn't see across the road for exhaust smoke. By the crossing there used to be a cafe, which became a store, where we are told the bus fare-takings were deposited. On the left hand side of the road the vertical cafe sign was sufficient to those in the street at that time a guarantee of a good snack or full meal, backed as it was by the resources and reputation of the Co-op in Derby.

Below left: Derby's main thoroughfare runs from the Cathedral at the northern end to the The Spot at the southern end, changing its name along the way from Irongate at the Cathedral to Cornmarket, at the junction with Market Place, and finally to St Peter's Street at the junction with Victoria Street. East of Irongate is Friar Gate, the Georgian area of the city. English landscape and portrait painter Joseph Wright (1734 - 1797), known as 'Wright of Derby', and acclaimed as 'the first professional painter to express the spirit of the Industrial Revolution', was born in Irongate. This turn of the century photograph of Irongate recalls a time that has now all but passed from living memory. Only a few

centenarians can still recall the days when tramlines still existed on the roadbed and horse drawn vehicles rather than cars and lorries filled our streets. Though many were glad to see the end of horse, which unlike cars bit at one end and kicked at the other, many more were sorry to see them go. Gardeners keen to feed their roses were always pleased to be able to pop out in the road with a bucket and shovel to collect free manure. Inexplicably it was the rag and bone men who retained their horses and carts longer than any other trade. Even as late as the 1970s the incomprehensible cry of the rag and bone man with his flat bed cart could till be heard around the streets.

Below: It might have been wartime, but two aspects of normal life continued unabated – religion and commerce. Here they run side by side as two old Derby names dominate this picture of Victoria Street, taken around 1940. Religion was catered for here by the Victoria Street Congregational Church, seen in the centre of this picture. The building shown was demolished in 1962 and a new church building erected as changes went on nationally to the denomination. In 1972 the Congregational Union of England and Wales and the Presbyterian Church of England were joined to form the United Reformed Church and the Victoria Street Congregational Church, Derby, which had been rebuilt in 1964, became the Central United Reformed Church. The other name is one of commerce with the famous old department store Ranby's, which had been established many years before and which was taken over in the early 1970s by the Debenham Group. Though the old store may have gone, the name Ranby's still lives on in the name of a well known pub in Green Lane.

Top right: The Castle and Falcon in The Morledge, seen centre-picture, was afterwards demolished and rebuilt on the corner of East Street, which was formerly Bag Lane. On the left on the sky line is the ice factory of the Derby Cold Storage Company. The efficiency of this facility was inadvertently put to the test by the photographer who was commissioned to take some shots of the interior of the refrigeration plant. With his blood pumping well and his adrenaline high, he was eager to get on with taking photographs of the frozen fish and meat, although he was dressed for normal outdoor temperature. 'Will you be alright in there?' the manager asked. 'Right as a trivet,' answered Hubert, checking his camera, and went inside the store. He endured it for about three minutes, by which time he was chilled to the bone and his joints were stiffening. Fortunately, no long term harm was done, and he continues to take historic photographs, though not in 'freezers'.

Right: Any city centre is bound to be busy, but with bus station, market and the Eagle Centre nearby, Morledge is surely going to be one of the busiest parts. And it always has been as this picture from 1947 clearly demonstrates. While the traffic may be light, it is obviously taken at what might be described as rush hour judging by the number of people shown at the bottom right of the junction of Morledge and Albert Street. Many of them appear to be queueing, probably for buses, as at that time that was the easiest and quickest way to cross the city. How many people today would also venture through the centre on a bike, like the lone cyclist alongside the bus in the centre of the picture?

Below: Looking somewhat dilapidated in this picture thought to be taken in the late 1950s or early 1960s these buildings and St Alkmund's churchyard were demolished in 1967 to make way for the St Alkmund's Way road traffic system. The picture shows the chancel of St Alkmund's Church on the left, with St Mary's Gate going off to the right and Darley Lane straight on. The Lamb Inn, shown on the right, had existed since 1835 in a late medieval building. A sheep roast had been held here to celebrate the end of the Crimean War and the beers served were brewed on the premises. The pub was

sold to Offilers Ales and closed in 1967 to make way for the Inner Ring Road, St Alkmund's Way. There are only six churches in England dedicated to Saint Alkmund, who was born in 774 in northern England as a British prince. The church, on Bridge Gate, was rebuilt in 1843 by H I Stevens at a cost of £7,700 and was demolished in 1967 to make way for the ring road, which now bears its name.

Right: A busy Market Place in the 1960s. The view is not much different to that of the present day. Saint Alkmunds spire can be seen to the left of the Cathedral. Dominating the picture is the Barlow & Taylor building which was built in 1925. The building to the right of Barlow & Taylor is Wine Vaults, built in 1734, it was demolished in 1970 to make way for the Derby Assembly Rooms.

Right: The photograph was taken in 1959 before the power station was demolished. The view looks up Full Street from the traffic island at the junction with Derwent Street. On the right is the police station with the power station behind it to the left. Full Street is in the centre, with the tower of the cathedral on the left. The street, which goes to the left of the half-timbered building, led up to the market square. All of the buildings on the left have since been demolished and the multi-storey car park and Assembly Rooms complex now stands in their place. Full Street's name appears to have come from the woollen industry. Walker Lane was a reference to local industry of the time. A "walker" was a fuller who cleaned off whitened woollen cloth by trampling on it with his bare feet. Nearly opposite Walker Lane was Full Street, that is Fullers' Street or Fulling Street, close by the riverside where the "walkers" were employed, and fuller's earth, a type of absorbent clay was something which was much used by them.

arket places tend to be among the most important parts of any ancient city or town and Derby is no exception. This picture of the Market Place shows the magnificent Guildhall, with its distinctive clocktower. The Guildhall was built in 1828 by Habershon, but after a fire was later remodelled in 1841-2 by Duesbury and Lee. They gave the Guildhall its central tower and domed cap. The two reliefs by John Bell on either side of the main bay show "Scientia" and "Industria". Inside, the council chamber, with a fine coffered ceiling, was converted into a theatre in 1971 and much used by local theatrical societies. The other rooms are often used by clubs and as studios for local artists. A covered walkway under the Guildhall leads to the Market Hall, dating back to 1864. The War Memorial in front of the Guildhall was designed by C A Thompson and built in the Market Place by A G Walker in 1924. It was also the scene of floral tributes following the death of Princess Diana. The statue of Michael Thomas Bass, MP for Derby between 1848 and 1883, originally stood in the Market Place. He funded the building of the library and museum. The statue, made by J E Boehm in 1884, now stands in Museum Square outside these buildings.

Right: This photograph was taken from The Council House balcony, looking down Derwent Street onto the Market Place square. The most prominent building is the Guildhall, with its distinctive copper- domed clock-tower where lots of couples used to meet. On the left side street corner, by the zebra crossing, is Phillipsons store, which was the forerunner of garden-centre establishments. Beyond the bus picking up passengers at the bus shelter is the Market Place, which has long been a passenger ascending/descending point, from the days of two wheeled handsome cabs and four wheeled 'growlers'. Thrown the years the Market Place has seen horse drawn trams and buses, electric trams and trolleys, diesel and petrol buses. The Market Place is where cycling clubs would meet to set off for the day; likewise the Ramblers Association, and the trippers. It was also the assembly place for the floats in the processions going to Derby carnivals at Markeaton Park.

Below: Derwent Street crosses the River Derwent on Exeter Bridge in this picture taken in the early 1950s. It shows distant buildings and bridges that are no longer there. The long bridge beyond the river island is the old towpath connecting both arms of the Derby Canal on either side of the river, The 14-mile canal was commissioned in 1793 and opened in 1796. The canal was never nationalised. It was abandoned in 1964, but now the Derby Canal Society is trying to restore it. Beyond towpath bridge is the cast iron bridge that linked the cattle market with Meadow Lane. On the right is The Council House, which was designed by C H Aslin, the founder of the City Architect's Department who also built the bus station and redeveloped the whole area around the River Gardens. It is a brick building with stone dressings and a giant portico facing the roundabout opposite the Market Place. The site was cleared as part of Derby's 1930s Central Improvement Scheme. Exeter Bridge which carries Derwent Street over the river is a single span concrete bridge which was also built in 1931 by Aslin, and replaced an earlier stone one. It was opened on 13th March 1931 by Herbert Morrison MP. The original Exeter Bridge was completed in 1850, became a "passing" bridge for traffic and tramways in 1929, but when it re-opened in 1931, it had no tramlines on it as the tram programme abandonment plan was under way.

Pedestrians now wander down Cornmarket, but it was not always so as the area was blocked off to traffic in 1990s. There was always plenty of light, however, as this picture taken in 1955 indicates. The street lights shine brightly, the bus is brilliantly lit and despite the darkness some of the fine Victorian architecture can still be clearly seen. The Kardomah Café on the left may provide a welcome for the people pictured below the sign, but on the right is an advertisement which clearly indicates this picture is from a time gone by as "Player's Please" would definitely not be allowed today.

Right: This picture shows St Mary's Bridge around 1966. The structure seen here leads to St Mary's Roman Catholic Church and was constructed over the River Derwent by Thomas Harrison of Chester in 1789-94 to replace a much earlier medieval bridge. Although many of the buildings seen here have gone, the pub seen on the right of the picture is still serving patrons. A feature of the bridge is one of Derby's most well-known historical buildings, the St Mary's Bridge Chapel. This is the oldest chapel in Derby and one of only six such "bridge" chapels remaining in the country. These chapels were built to provide revenue by the collection of tolls from those persons who wished to cross the bridge as well as providing a place for travellers to pray and seek blessings for their journey. The remains of the former medieval bridge can still just be seen at the base of the chapel. The chapel itself dates back as far as 1275 and underwent restoration in 1930. Saint Mary's Bridge is also notorious as the site of the murder of the Derby Martyrs, three Catholic priests named Robert Ludlum, Nicholas Garlick and Richard Sympson. On July 24, 1588, they were taken to St Mary's Bridge where they were hung drawn and quartered. Their dismembered bodies were then displayed on poles on the approaches to the bridge.

Left: Looking at the picture taken of The Morledge from Cockpit Hill in 1936 you see a Derby in the midst of change, with evolution moved into top gear by a new progressive need to do things, go places and see things. There is the timeless backdrop of All Saints Church (a cathedral from 1927). To its right is St Alkmunds with its fine spire and St Mary's just behind it. Moving forwards in time, in the centre left of the picture you see the chimneys overtopping the generating plant of Derby's electrical power station, built in the 1920s and demolished in the 1970s. Nearer still to present day, the trolley bus presence is a growing sign of Derby's modernity, but single decker buses have already appeared, (from memory) in a cream and green livery. From the photograph, what is the biggest contrast in transportation, would you say? The motorbike and side-car combination against the milk-float, or what about the same milk float just about to pass the char-a-banc coming in the opposite direction? Did you ever go on a works trip in the old style 'Sharrarbang' to Alton Towers, or come home from Tutbury with a piece of cut crystal glass after watching the Horn Dance at Abbots Bromley (first Monday after September 4th)? Did your husband take you shopping in town on Saturdays in the sidecar? Maybe you moved a bit further away from the next street to the factory with your new mobility! The 'Johnny on the Corner' in the Panama hat was a familiar sight in 1936, scratching a living in hard times for some. He wasn't interested in the liner 'Queen Mary' taking the rich and famous on the Atlantic run to America; more likely he was disturbed to learn, as he stood there on this day, that there was a place called Jarrow full of unemployed shipbuilding workers who were marching the 291 miles to London and might as well have stayed at home.

Above: This intriguing view, taken where The Cornmarket meets St James Street in the 1930s poses as many questions as it answers, of people if not of the place. Looking directly down towards Market Head, you have a clear view of Barlow Taylor and Company's building which, (as you will probably know if you have ever arranged a mortgage in Derby) became the Derbyshire Building Society. When the picture was taken the Old Wine Vaults pub, which disappeared in 1971, was next to Barlow Taylor, and beneath the concealing canopies at pavement level would be The Midlands Drapery store at the corner of St Peter's and East Streets. In the foreground, on the left hand side, the policeman on point duty has his attention divided between looking at the photographer with his heavy professional camera on a tripod, and the flat-capped pedestrian wearing a heavy Crombie overcoat flapping open on a hot summer's day. The policeman on traffic duty is fairly close to Barclays Bank, inside the St James building. Down the road on the right another watchful policeman has dismounted his bicycle so he can study the situation more closely, just like yourself.

Above: This is Derby Market Place taken from the Guildhall in the 1950s, as we can tell from the cars parked in the centre. The building on the far right is the Old Assembly Rooms which were built for social gatherings which gave the young people opportunity to enjoy dances and soirees, parties and performances in an easily chaperoned situation, as well as its prime purpose as a meeting place for polite society. The Old Assembly Rooms featured tea rooms on the ground floor. and a large ballroom on the first floor. It was a favourite venue for performances by the Derby Choral Society Post war it was renovated in 1948 and the roof was replaced six years later. The fire of 1963 provided good reason to build anew. The new Assembly Rooms are now behind the war memorial, as seen from this angle of the camera. Work started in 1973 and the project was completed in time for a royal opening by Queen Elizabeth the Queen Mother on 9th November 1977, the year Derby achieved City status. The cenotaph in the foreground typifies every village, town and city in the country which has its war memorial to those who died for Britain. The inscription here reads 'For Faith and Hope and Righteousness'.

Top right: Cornmarket always has been a thriving city centre street, which was eventually pedestrianised in the 1990s. The picture shows the junction with Market Place, taken in 1964, and is dominated by a policeman on point duty – a rare sight these days, but fairly common back then, judging by the volume of traffic he has to deal with. The shops pictured include the Kardomah Café, John Field, jeweller, John Temple and Cope & Taylor, Chemists. Cornmarket still contains much fine Victorian architecture. Along the streets today you will find well known high street stores, some housed in Victorian buildings built as a huge department store where the staff slept over the shops. Cornmarket is also home to grand old bank and building society buildings and reminders of the clockmakers, which have all played their part in the area's history. It still contains various banking institutions. Local wool dyer and businessman Robert Liversage originally lived in a building on the site where Samuel's is located. He donated much of the money needed to build the city's cathedral tower.

Right: Trees line the road in this view of Friar Gate and the Friar Gate Bridge taken in the late 1950s. It shows the route into the city centre with not only trees, but a row of elegant Georgian houses on the left. "Dr Southern's House" is the one with the ball decorations adorning the roof, near to the Great Northern Railway Bridge. This iron, single-span bridge was constructed by Andrew Handyside and Company Ltd, ironfounders of Derby in 1877. The bridge has "lacy cast-iron balustrade and spandrels, and arches of lattice construction". The company specialised in ornamental fountains and major engineering works.

AT LEISURE

The area around Rykneld Recreation Ground has been a popular spot over many decades. It was not just summertime activities there. While this picture shows fun in the sun, the Rec or Ricky Rec as it was known to many could also provide fun in the winter too. It has a large steep hill and in the winter when it had snowed this was the place to come with a sledge, or failing that anything that could be used to slide on even just plastic sheets. But this picture takes us back to the lazy, hazy days of summer when there was a paddling pool close to the recreation ground, which was very popular with kids cooling off on fine sunny days. But in the 1950s a polio epidemic sweeping the country was though to be water-borne and mothers in Derby refused to let their children anywhere near such places, so the activities came to an end.

Right: The Arboretum was donated to Derby in 1840 by Joseph Strutt, a former Mayor and member of a prominent family of local industrialists. Strutt, a noted philanthropist, was grateful to the working people of Derby for the part they had played in helping him and his family amass their fortune, and wanted to express his thanks by providing the much welcomed park. Joseph Strutt commissioned John Claudius Loudon to design the park, and Loudon adapted Strutt's original plans for a botanical garden and pleasure grounds to his own vision. Work on the Arboretum began in July 1839, and was completed in time for the grand opening which took place on 16th September 16. The occasion was marked by a parade from the Market

Place in the centre of Derby to the new park. The park initially charged for admission, in order to pay for its upkeep. However, admission was free on Sundays and on Wednesdays (which had been adopted as half day closing in Derby). This mean that the poor classes, who had limited leisure time could gain free access when they actually had the time to do so: in effect, the park was paid for by those who had time and money to spare. Charging was finally abolished in 1882. A scene from Ken Russell's 1969 Oscar winning film Women in Love was shot at the Arboretum. The scene had the Aslin designed band stand with a brass band playing whilst Oliver Reed, Alan Bates and Glenda Jackson spoke.

Bottom left: It was not all work for employees of the Derby Corporation Omnibus Department and outings and trips were popular. This picture taken around 1950 is believed to show a department outing to New Brighton for female staff members. The coach, hired from Barton's, is parked outside Ranby's department store, opposite the store's offices in Victoria Street. Ranby's was rebuilt in modern style in the early 1960s and then taken over by Debenham's, while Woolworth's, which can be seen in the background moved to the new Eagle Centre in the mid-1970s. The Omnibus Department offices were in a building which originally opened 1904 as the Tramway offices. Once the bus department took over, the shop on the street level was used as an enquiry office and crew room. The building is now the Post Office.

Below: Tiffany's dance hall and nightclub was still in full swing in Babington Lane when this picture was taken in 1970. But it was just one of many incarnations for the building which started life as the Grand Theatre. Over the years it has been various nightclubs, not only Tiffany's, but also the Locarno, Confettis, Ritzy's, Eclipse and McClusky's. The Grand Theatre was opened on land that was formerly the gardens of Babington House. It closed in 1950, becoming Tiffany's dance hall and The Eclipse/Progress night club. The view looks down Gower Street. The theatre had opened in 1886 but burned down within a month of opening. It was rebuilt and reopened in 1904. Gower Street was once called Blood Lane. McClusky's closed down in 2006 and the premises reopened on 19th July, 2007 as May Sum, a Chinese restaurant.

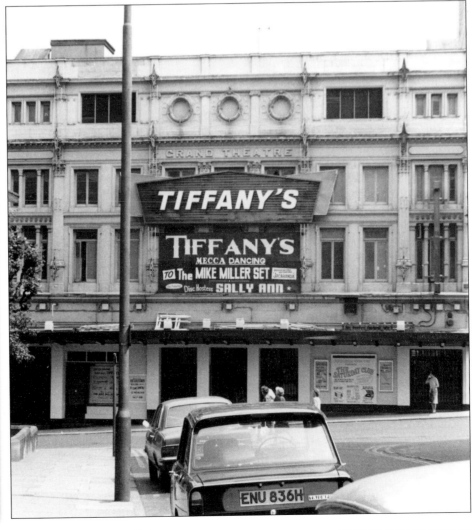

Below: Long before EasyJet and Ryanair took to the skies, Derby had its own airline jetting people off to the sun. This advertisement from the early 1960s also indicates that Derby also had its own airport. Derby Airways changed its name to British Midland Airways in 1964. It flew from an airfield at Bumaston, known officially as Derby Airport. Go by air and add two days to your holiday was another advertising slogan of Derby Airways. An early traveller to Ostend in 1957 recalls: "Derby Airport did not have metalled runways and so we hurtled across the grass field before taking off. "I was amazed at how smooth it seemed, once we were airborne, compared to the rattle and vibration on the runways. "We then made our way to Elmdon Airport, Birmingham, to go through customs, as there were none at Derby." It was in 1938 that Air Schools Limited was established, specialising in flying instruction for RAF pilots. More than 10 years later it diversified operations and formed Derby Aviation and Wolverhampton Aviation based at Burnaston airfield, near Derby. Both companies offered ad-hoc passengers and cargo charters with Derby Aviation specialising in civil aircraft maintenance and aircraft brokerage. The year 1958 marked the start of inclusive tour holidays to France, Spain, Italy, Austria and Switzerland. A year later, Derby Aviation was renamed Derby Airways and the network expanded to cover more UK destinations. In 1964, Derby Airways changed its name to British Midland Airways Ltd then to Airlines of Britain Holdings PLC in 1987; and to British Midland plc in 1997. It is now known as BMI.

Bottom right: Flights to the sun began to take off in the 1960s. While the destination of this happy group is a mystery, it is no mystery with which airline they were flying. British Midland Airways, now known as BMI is one of the success stories of Derbyshire. It began life in 1938 as Air Schools Ltd, which specialised in training RAF pilots. In 1949 the company became known as Derby Aviation and offered passenger and cargo charter services. In the fifties, the company ended RAF training and expanded its passenger routes across the UK and Europe and its cargo routes worldwide. The company became known as British Midland Airways in 1964, and merged with Invica Airways in 1969. In 1979, the company celebrated one million passengers carried in a year. In 1986, the airline changed its name to British Midland and in the following year it introduced its frequent flyer scheme, the Diamond Club. In 2002 bmibaby was launched and in 2003, the airline became known as BMI.

FLY DERBY and meet the sun!
FLY DERBY from DERBY AIRPORT
DERBY AIRWAYS
DERBY AIRPORT
Telephone: Etwall 521 OR YOUR LOCAL TRAVEL AGENCY
A MEMBER OF THE BRITISH INDEPENDENT AIR TRANSPORT ASSOCIATION

Left: When this picture was taken in 1977, the Talk of the Midlands was at the height of its short-lived existence. It was an entertainment-based nightclub venue, where stars performed in cabaret. The artist advertised on the billboard outside the club at the time of this picture was comedian Ken Dodd and some of the others who appeared at the venue included Matt Munro, Dave Allen, Les Dawson, Ella FitzGerald and Jack Jones. The Talk of the Midlands tried to maintain a dignified, stylish appeal, with ladies having to wear long dresses and men suits and ties. The building on Mill Street was originally a cinema which opened in August 1928. In 1981 it was converted to Gossips nightclub and was later owned by the Derby Students Union and then called The Riverside Health Club. It was demolished in February 2003.

Right: The Regal Cinema on East Street, part of the ABC cinema group, first opened on 27th June 1938 and closed its doors for the last time on 14th July 1984. Almost ironically the last film shown was 'That's Entertainment'. The ABC (Associated British Cinemas) Group had its origins in the activities of former solicitor John Maxwell in Scotland. Starting in the film industry as an exhibitor with one cinema in Glasgow, and realising that in order to have any bargaining power with film distributors it was necessary for him to have greater booking power, Maxwell began acquiring ever more cinemas. He then decided that, in order to ensure a suitable and adequate supply of films for them on reasonable terms, he needed to secure some control over distribution. In 1923 Maxwell acquired a distributing company called Wardour Films Ltd. with headquarters in London. Maxwell, believing that the British industry should be freed from American domination, considered that the way to free it was to create a completely integrated and wholly British concern which would undertake production, distribution and exhibition. In 1926 he formed a company called British International Pictures Ltd. (BIP) for that purpose. BIP acquired Associated British Cinemas Ltd. (ABC), a company which had been formed by Maxwell to take over his own cinemas. It became the British integrated organisation, active in production, distribution and exhibition, which Maxwell had sought to create - though from 1941 onwards part of it was owned by the United States company, Warner Bros. Pictures.

Left: Hundreds of Derby businesses have disappeared down the decades, many of which were very well known local names. Joicies the bakers based in East Street and the Market Hall was one such name. If the baker's advert from the 1950s is anything to go by, no marriage could survive on harmonious terms without a housewife making regular trips to Joicies. In those un-politically correct days men and women knew their places: men were the breadwinners but wives did the shopping. Could advertisers get away with this sort of sexist campaign now? Surely not. Whether or not men really did prefer crusty bread however was always questionable. The bread-slicing machine had been around since 1928, and sliced bread was making heavy inroads into sales of the traditional loaf. Today it seems almost impossible to believe that sliced bred was once a rarity. On reason why sliced bread had been relatively slow to catch on was the fact that it needed careful packaging. Wartime paper shortages meant that the uncut loaf continued in popularity rather longer than might have otherwise been the case. On the other hand perhaps the fact that the bread-slicing machine had been invented by the German sounding Otto Frederick Rohwedder had prejudiced the British public. By the early 1960s however industrial scale bread making and 'slice and wrap' machines in huge bakeries were already driving many smaller businesses to closure. Now long gone, Joicies began in business in the 1930s and at that time were particularly noted for their biscuits.

Derby's Aquabelles brought a touch of Hollywood glamour to town in days gone by. They entertained crowds in this region and beyond in the 40s and 50s, Eva Lingard, pictured right, was the charismatic founder and leader of the water ballet group of glamorous synchronised swimmers, 16 to 18 beautiful girls who were always dressed in swimsuits. Eva Lingard had been an outstanding competitive swimmer in her youth and when she became a teacher and coach she broke new ground in water-based entertainment by establishing the water ballet in Derby in 1945. She was prompted to do this after seeing the popularity of aquatic star Esther Williams in her swimming movies. The idea was to bring a bit of Hollywood glamour to Derby and she certainly did that with graceful musical water ballet displays, which attracted huge crowds to Derby's Queen Street Swimming baths. At the time

swimming galas were very popular and held regularly on Saturday evenings with swimming competitions, water polo matches, diving displays, Eva Lingard thought the displays by the girls would add to the interest. In those early days it

was more flotation displays and water somersaults with the girls doing rhythmical exercises on the side of the pool before, one by one, elegantly diving into the water where they went into their acrobatic routines. Female applicants wishing to join the elite group, as well as having to look good, also had to be strong swimmers. They were not only taught the routines in the water, led by Vera Dickens, but also how to glide when walking on the poolside and how to do their hair and make-up. Eva Lingard was born in 1908 and won numerous swimming races along with a host of titles and medals. She became a Midlands champion and the star of the pool in Derby, winning the highly coveted Derby Hospital Cup on two occasions. After her own competitive days were over, she coached young girls in Derby and became a well-known swimming teacher for many local schools. She met her husband, James at the old Reginald Street Swimming Baths when he was taking a dip while on a visit from Lancashire and she was there for her daily training routine. The Aquabelles continued until 1960 when the group disbanded. Water ballet later went on to be known as synchronised swimming and eventually became an Olympic sport.

WARTIME

Is it raining out there? There are smiles on the faces of the adults trying out the Anderson air raid shelter, but not on the faces of the kids who were helping to build this particular shelter near Traffic Street in 1938 or 1939. It was just one of a vast number of the home made shelters issued by the Government to ordinary people throughout the country. Sir John Anderson, who was in charge of Air Raid Precautions (ARP), commissioned a small and cheap shelter that could be erected in people's gardens. Within a few months nearly one and a half million of what became known as Anderson shelters were distributed to people living in areas expected to be bombed. Made from six curved sheets bolted together at the top, with steel plates at either end, and measuring 6ft 6in by 4ft 6in (1.95m by 1.35m) the shelter could accommodate six people. These shelters were half buried in the ground with earth heaped on top. The entrance was protected by a steel shield and an earthen blast wall. Anderson shelters were given free to poor people. Men who earned more than £5 a week could buy one for £7. Soon after the outbreak of the Second World War in September 1939, over two million families had shelters in their gardens.Anderson shelters were dark and damp and people were reluctant to use them at night. In low-lying areas they tended to flood and sleeping was difficult as they did not keep out the sound of the bombings. Another problem was that the majority of people living in industrial areas did not have gardens where they could erect their shelters, as may have been the case in the one shown in the picture.

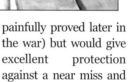

Above: It is thought that this picture is in the newly constructed but not yet connected section of drainage pipe under Harvey Road (Allenton to Alvaston), which was used as an air raid shelter. Britain declared war on Germany on the 3rd September, 1939. The country had been expecting war and many preparations had been made leading up to this day. In the long hot summer of 1939 people witnessed the impending and eventual outbreak of World War II. The extended school summer holiday saw furious activity in the deserted school playgrounds and verdant public parklands. Mechanical excavators were busy digging trenches in these playgrounds, in almost every city park, and in many sports grounds. (people were also digging Anderson shelters and Morrison Shelters at their own homes). The aim of all this activity was to provide underground refuges for the population. This war would bring a new threat - aerial attack by bombs of 500kg and more - the front line was not to be a muddy field in some far off land. These trenches were to be known as 'Public Underground Air Raid Shelters'. Size would vary greatly, from a humble 50 person shelter to much larger work's shelters. Some shelters were basic, offering merely protection from the German bombers overhead and somewhere to sit and answer the call of nature. Others rose to the luxury of bunks and a canteen. By late 1940, virtually everybody living in town or city, was hopefully no more than five minutes from an underground refuge. These air raid shelters would be no protection against a direct hit (as would be so painfully proved later in the war) but would give excellent protection against a near miss and perhaps more importantly against flying debris such as roof slates, masonry, glass and shrapnel. The shelter seen here is being inspected by Alderman C R Bates, Alderman A E Moult, Chief Constable of Derby, Wing Comm. Hodsoll (Inspector General for ARP), Lord Trent (Regional Commissioner for the North Midlands) and Major G Lidbury (Senior Regional ARP Officer for Nottingham).

Top right: The second world war may have begun with its tanks, ships and planes but that didn't mean that there was no place left for the humble horse. Soldiers were stationed at Derby Racecourse during the war and are pictured here with the horses they were assigned to care for. Though the internal combustion engine had been around for half a century real horsepower was far from being replaced. During the war years horses and carts became an increasingly common sight, and motor vehicles rather rarer, as petrol became in increasingly short supply. As for warhorses, well there was no older war horse than Churchill himself. Winston was a former cavalry man and had participated in the British Army's last full cavalry charge at the battle of Omdurman in 1898. Though the army would have little use for cavalry charges in the second world war it did have use for

thousands of horses as draught animals and for parade ground duties. Happily most British horses survived the war uninjured – only a generation earlier however millions of horses had died in the first world war as they pulled heavy guns and other equipment to the front line trenches.

Left: With the threat of war looming an Act was passed creating the Auxiliary Fire Service, which on the outbreak of war saw the AFS members working alongside the regular fireman. The Blitz started from late summer in 1940 and saw widespread devastation all over the country. Thousands of men and machinery were called in to deal with the fires. Tragically, during the Blitz in Derby - 25th June, 1940, to 9th July, 1941 - 28 civilians were killed in their homes, workplaces and in the streets.

Left: The lady in this picture has every right to have a worried and serious look. The photograph was taken in September 1939 soon after war was declared and she is carrying back to her home something designed to be part of Britain's defence system. She is holding special blackout paper for the "Blackout" Scheme. From the beginning of the war, precautions were taken to "black-out" all lights. This became essential as it soon became clear that most bombing raids would take place at night. It was thought that a light, even from one house, would be used as a target by an enemy plane on which it could drop its bombs. Each night everyone in the country had to make sure that not one chink of light escaped from the windows and doors of their homes. Heavy curtains or blinds could be effective but some windows were simply painted over or covered with cardboard or thick paper, such as this lady is carrying, for the duration of the war.

Below: The Wartime Meals Division encouraged the setting up of industrial canteens, and lent local authorities money to start British Restaurants for the public. Meals eaten away from home, whether in expensive West End restaurants or industrial canteens, were 'off ration' and a popular alternative with people who could afford them. The conspicuous ability of the rich to

enjoy almost pre-war levels of gastronomy at top hotels led to such resentment from the public at large that the government prevented restaurants charging more than 5/- a meal from 1942. This curbed the most ostentatious examples, though it did not completely solve the problem. A typical dinner in 1942 consisted of roast beef and two vegetables, treacle pudding, bread and butter and coffee and cost only 11d. Standards varied, but the best were greatly appreciated and had a large regular clientele. British Restaurants were run by local authorities, who set them up in a variety of different premises such as schools and church halls as well as established cafes. They were open to all, but mainly served office and industrial workers, although Derby's 'City Restaurant', seen here, mainly catered to those who did not have access to a works canteen. By the end of the war there were 2,000 British Restaurants serving more than half a million meals a day.

Bottom right: World War II brought about major change for women in the services. In December 1941 the government passed the National Service Act (No 2), which made provision for the conscription of women. At first only childless widows and single women 20 to 30 years old were called up, but later the age limit was expanded to 19 to 43 (50 for WWI veterans). As well as conscription and the usual clerical and domestic duties, women did a much wider variety of jobs than they did in World War I, such as driving and maintaining vehicles, manning anti-aircraft guns and RADAR stations, ferrying aircraft from factories to airfields, deciphering coded German messages in secret naval communications units and working as spies in the Special Operations Executive (SOE). As part of the conscription requirement women had to chose whether to enter the armed forces or work in farming or industry. Many women decided that they would work in a factory. By December 1943 one in three factory workers was female and they were building planes, tanks, guns and making bullets needed for the war. Women worked in all manner of production ranging from making ammunition to uniforms to aeroplanes. The hours they worked were long and some women had to move to where the factories were. Those who moved away were paid more. Skilled women could earn £2.15 a week. (Although men doing the same work were paid more!). The war in Europe ended in May 1945. At this time there were 460,000 women in the military and over 6.5 million in civilian war work.

Bottom: The Women's Voluntary Service was founded as a Civil Defence auxiliary unit in 1938. The WVS gained much experience in providing emergency meals during the second world war, often using the most primitive equipment. WVS mobile canteens served the forces both at home and abroad. During the war years the WVS gained an unforgettable reputation amongst both members of the armed forces and those whose homes had been bombed, always ensuring that cups of tea, sandwiches and cakes were provided exactly where they were needed. When the war ended however members of the WVS had acquired a taste for public service and were unwilling simply to close shop. Distributing Meals on Wheels on a regular basis to needy people, particularly the elderly, after the war was a new challenge, but one the organisation readily adapted to. In the first six months of 1958, the year when this photograph was taken, the WVS delivered 75,000 such meals - the first course always piping hot from 'Hot Lock'

containers. In this picture the WVS are looking delighted at the acquisition of two brand new vans. The fully-fitted vehicles named Cowan and Hanover are gaining the seal of approval. Things had moved a long way from the immediate post-war years when members often delivered meals in their own vehicles.

Left: War had been declared, and every citizen of Britain, young and old, male and female, was called upon to put his or her back into the war effort. Those who did not go into military service of one kind or another worked in factories, dug for victory, gave up their aluminium baths and saucepans, joined organisations and aided in any way they could. These boys from were not going to be left out; they might be too young to fight but while there were sandbags to be filled they were going to do their bit to protect their school building. Thousands of sandbags were used during World War II to protect the country and its beautiful civic buildings.

Below: It was possibly the acute wartime shortages of food and supplies which made doctors, health workers and mothers alike very aware of the health of the new generation, and children were carefully weighed, measured and immunised against the illnesses that had at one time meant disfigurement or even death. A vaccine for polio, the scourge of former years which left behind its terrible mark of wasted and useless limbs, only came later, however. American scientist Jonas Edward Salk developed a vaccine in 1955, and an oral vaccine was produced in 1960. The vaccines brought the dreaded disease under control and today polio is rarely seen. On a day to day basis, vitamins were vital to the health of children, and long before the advent of the cod liver oil capsule, the recommended spoonful of cod liver oil was administered to the youngest children every day in schools and nurseries around the country during the 1940s. Children might have screwed up their noses at the fishy taste, but the nourishing cod liver oil went a long way towards keeping them healthy. The vitamin-packed orange juice was far more palatable, and artful mothers would often use the orange juice as a bribe: no cod liver oil, no orange juice. Following hard on the heels of the oil, the juice took away the distinctive taste that was disliked by so many children.

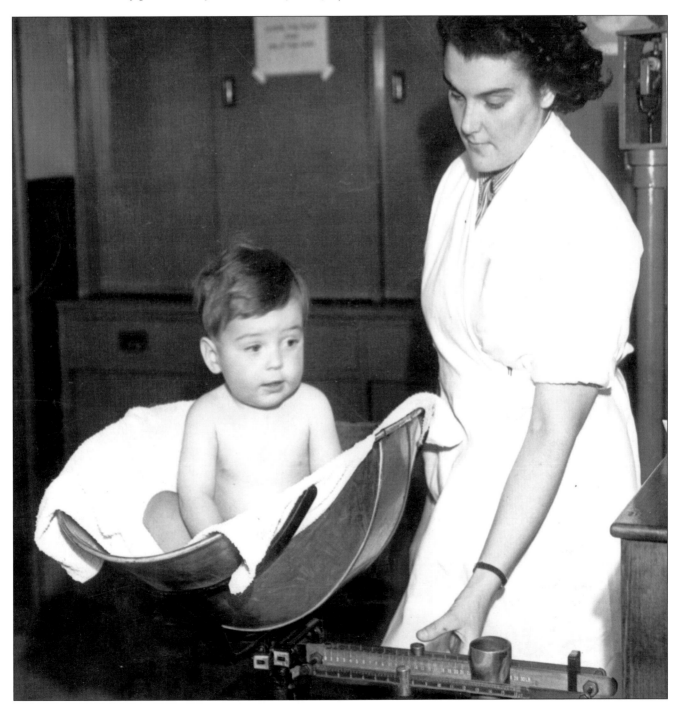

Mertrux - Mercedes-Benz in Derby

Derby's much-respected Mercedes-Benz main dealer Mertrux Ltd has roots which go back to a chance encounter in London's Dorchester Hotel in 1970. Burton on Trent motor dealer Bert Deacon and his Truck Sales Manager E D 'Don' Marshall had been looking at commercial vehicles at that year's Motor Show. Over dinner they discussed the possibility of obtaining a franchise to sell Mercedes-Benz trucks.

Bert Deacon had been in the motor trade since 1932. Don Marshall had joined him as a tractor salesman in 1963 after having earlier been a farm worker, working for Lord Burton at Rangemoor, Burton on Trent.

Mercedes' commercial vehicles were first produced as long ago as 1896. The 'birth certificate' of the world's first automobile was the humble patent number 37435 issued by the Imperial Patent Office in Berlin in January 1886 to a factory owner Karl Benz. In that same year Gottlieb Daimler was conducting trials with a 'motor carriage'. Quite independently these two men laid the foundations for the age of the motor car.

In 1898 a Viennese businessman called Emil Jellinek raced a Daimler Phoenix car in the Tour de Nice naming the vehicle after his eight year old daughter, Mercedes. In 1900 he ordered 36 similar vehicles on condition that he be granted an agency to sell them and that the cars should bear his daughter's name.

By 1902 the name had caught on so well that the company, now Daimler-Motoren-Gesellschaft took out a trade mark on it. The Mercedes-Benz name was born in 1926 with the merger of Daimler with the Benz company.

In England in 1970 Mertrux then known as Autofair became only the third Mercedes-Benz commercial dealer in Britain, opening its doors for business in Burton on Trent on 3rd January 1971. £15,000 was scraped together to get the new business off the ground. It was a great deal of money then - but that personal commitment would be more than justified with sales which would eventually exceed £50 million a year. Don Marshall's team gave it everything. At a time when demonstrators were almost unheard of in the truck business there was hardly a day when Autofair's 32 ton LPS1418 truck was not out on the road being shown to potential customers.

The very first truck order came from Eric Skeet of Draycott Transport in Burton: at a cost of £6,250 it was no small investment, but it was to become the first of several Mercedes to join their fleet.

*Top: Mertrux's showroom in the 1980s. **Left:** Ilkeston-based J&P Transport with their new Mercedes-Benz Actros supplied in 2007 by Mertrux from their new site at Mansfield.*

Bert Deacon was pleased to report to the company board at the first year end that Don Marshall and his team had sold over 70 vehicles. 'We'll double that next year' he said. And they did.

In 1971 Mercedes-Benz commercial vehicles were still rare on Britain's roads. The name meant prestige cars to most people. British truckers who drove to the continent however, had seen Mercedes trucks: many asked why can't I have a 'Merc'.

Autofair was amongst the first of several new franchises to be awarded in the first half of the 1970s.

Developments at Mercedes-Benz during this period included the introduction of a new generation of cab and the launch of a full range of 'V' formation engines.

Customers who tried out one Mercedes truck found themselves coming back again and again: Dave Shilton has now been using Mertrux vehicles for over thirty years, Mick Clark of MD Clark has similarly bought vehicles for more than two decades, as have Allegro Transport, Anthony & Spencer, Putzmeister, FP Walker Limited, Trent Insulations, Courtaulds Chemicals and Frank Wright of Ashbourne.

Top: An exterior view of the showroom in the early 1990s. ***Above:*** *Mertrux Commercial Sales, Service and Parts reception at Derby, newly redesigned in 2007.* ***Right:*** *And they keep coming back...Norman Smith hands over a new car to long standing customer Sandy Moore, (inset) and fifteen years later here they are again!*

Several people worked with Bert Deacon and Don Marshall, in their pre-Mercedes days and would come to be regarded as 'lifers'. Keith Godfrey, Parts Manager since 1982, had been with Bert and Don since he was an Apprentice Mechanic in 1962. Truck Workshop Foreman Chris Insley began as an Apprentice Mechanic in 1967, whilst amongst the firm's Fitters Paul Carey joined in 1975. The team would come to rank as one of the most experienced in the Mercedes truck dealership network.

Another 'old-timer' would be Martin Stock who became a Van and Truck Salesman in 1977 and would eventually become Mertrux's Commercial Vehicle Sales Director. In 1978 Ian Jones became known as 'six' because he was the sixth person to join the Parts Department; he had been helping his father John Jones on Saturday morning for years - John Jones had actually joined Bert Deacon in 1936 and was Mertrux Parts Manager until his retirement in 1982.

Other 'lifers' would come to include Simon Whittaker who joined the Parts Department in 1974 and Truck Service Advisor Robert Yates who joined in 1978 along with Ruth Brobyn who would become Don Marshall's Secretary.

Bert Deacon formally retired in 1978 although he retained a formal role as Chairman of the holding company.

In 1981 Mercedes Benz offered Autofair the passenger car franchise for Derby. This was an extra cause for celebration in the firm's 10th anniversary year.

A bigger business called for larger premises. On 1st September 1981 the whole organisation relocated from Burton to Chequers Road, Pentagon Island in Derby. With that move came a change of name to Mertrux (Derby) Ltd (it was to have been Mertrucks but an inspiration by Don Marshall's wife Hazel led to 'trucks' becoming 'trux').

The new premises cost half a million pounds and consisted of 6,000 sq ft of showrooms, 9,000 sq ft of workshops and a 3,000 sq ft parts department with meticulously planned offices and car park.

With the diversification into cars a Sales Manager was recruited to head up the new division. In September 1981 Norman Smith walked into a showroom with no lights, no carpet, no customers... and a stubbed finger. Norman had been involved in selling cars and motor cycles since the 1960s. Norman remembered his job interview well, not least because at its

Top: Ian Marshall handing over the keys of the first truck sold to Don Marshall, celebrating the Silver Jubilee at Mertrux Ltd. Right: The first truck sold now fully commissioned outside the new Mertrux site at Mansfield

conclusion Don Marshall presented him with a gift for his two children - a Charles and Diana engagement rug!

The year 1981 was one of recession yet despite that the firm still managed to sell its full quota of 80 vehicles, and achieved a turnover of £2 million.

The first passenger car sale was for a 200 Auto in champagne with light brown leather. It was bought by a Mr Lloyd of Derby at a cost of £9,000 and was run by him without fault for ten years. The car is now owned by Mertrux and carefully preserved. The first car to actually be delivered to a customer however was a 280E which went to another local businessman, Kevin Ellis, who has remained a loyal customer ever since.

Two years after beginning selling cars another long serving employee who joined the car division was Jon Rolley who would eventually become Commercial After Sales Manager.

The 1980s were a period for celebration for Mertrux. In 1983 Keith Godfrey's sterling performance in the Parts Department was nationally recognised by Mercedes-Benz with the award of Parts Manager of the Year. In 1987 Norman Smith was in the limelight as a finalist in the Pan-European Product Masters competition - a Mastermind-style quiz held in Berlin based on Mercedes product knowledge.

In 1987 work began on a new five-acre site just a few hundred yards from Pentagon Island on West Meadows Industrial Estate.

The deal was done in two days and the building up in just five months.

The greatest development of the decade was the introduction of the compact car in 1983. With the launch of the 190 model Mercedes opened up a mass car market for the first time and in the process brought one of the world's greatest marques within the price range of a whole new customer group. This helped lift Mercedes-Benz car sales in the UK up from 13,000 to over 23,000 in the following five years.

In 1987 the 200 series was launched to replace the hardy 123 and brought a new streamlining to Mercedes car design.

Finally, the decade saw the rebirth of the legendary SL, the ultimate grand tourer. The new SL was to be the first of a new generation of hi-tech computer-controlled cars: its hood mechanism alone boasted 13 different electronic functions.

Meanwhile on the commercial vehicle front there had been a number of important developments starting with

Top: *Mertrux's Leicester branch by night.* **Above:** *The award-winning Mercedes-Benz Sprinter on display at Mertrux's Leicester site.* **Right:** *In 2006 and 2007 Mertrux sponsored the Royal Show. Pictured is Don Marshall and his Female Championship Winner Charolais at the 2006 show.*

the 7.5 tonne 814 which became International Truck of the Year in 1984 scoring the highest marks awarded in its then nine year history winning the votes of all 13 international judges.

The year 1986 saw the introduction of Mercedes-Benz Powerliners the most powerful trucks yet to sport the famous three pointed star. The top of the range 1644S was the first to exceed the 400 bhp threshold. The Powerliner was a landmark vehicle featuring as standard the EPS gearbox which brought a new relaxed driving to Britain's truck drivers.

By the 1990s Mertrux had matured as a business, reaping the benefits of the care and patience put into it from birth. The decade began with a commitment by the company to achieving the rigorous quality standards required by ISO 9001: the painstaking programme was completed in just under six months: the first Mercedes-Benz dealership in the UK to receive certification.

Martin Stock was chosen by Mercedes-Benz for the prestigious title of Truck Sales Manager of the Year in 1990. That success was followed two years later with John Deakin winning the Accountant of the Year Award.

A bumper crop of awards came in 1993 with Martin Stock again becoming Truck Sales Manager of the Year and the

company being chosen from all the franchises in the UK to be acclaimed Truck Dealer of the Year. The occasion was marked by Mertrux hosting a tour of the Crown Derby factory and a Mercedes-Benz dinner for all winners at the Priest House Hotel in Castle Donington. That same year saw Mercedes seize a 10% share of the UK commercial vehicle market with sales of over 12,000 vans and trucks.

In its Silver Jubilee year Mertrux was again celebrating a triumph being awarded National Truck Dealer of the Year for the second time in three years.

The 1993 launch of the 'C' class brought the compact car into a new era. More and more people grew to appreciate the benefits of owning a 'Merc' not least because its famed residual value.

The launch of the 'E' class in 1995 represented another landmark in Mercedes design evolution - the vehicle's distinctive appearance reflecting a more youthful, avant-garde approach.

The addition of the SLK coupe, 'C' and 'E' Class estates and 'V' Class people carrier were important extensions of the range but the biggest revolution came in 1998 with the launch of the 'A' Class, the ultimate super-mini. The first ever Mercedes small car moved the company into the mass market in the

widest sense providing it with a product for every market sector.

With the appointment to the Board in 1994 of Martin Stock, Norman Smith and Joe O'Reilly the company recognised the invaluable contribution of its senior team members.

In 1996, to mark 25 years in business, Mertrux' long-standing customers were invited to a celebratory dinner attended by Stirling Moss which was held at Donington Park amidst the world's largest collection of Grand Prix Racing cars.

During that Silver Jubilee year Mertrux shared its success with others, donating a battery powered child sized Jeep to Derby's Children's Hospital, sponsoring the local children's football team the Etwall Comets and donating a table football to the charity Unique Coffee Bar. 2007 also brought a partnership between Mertrux and the Hawk Kawasaki team for the 2007 Bennetts British Superbike Championship. The dealership supplied two long bodied, high roofed Mercedes Vito 111 CDI vans to transport Hawk Kawasaki's ZX-10R

*Top: Gary Robson and Ian Marshall receive the Investor in People Awards, 2001. **Below left:** Mertrux donate a table football to charity 'Unique Coffee Bar' after the New Sprinter launch. **Below:** Mertrux Car Workshop and Service Team at Derby in 2007.*

machines for the championship's 13 rounds across England, Scotland and Ireland.

Mertrux is now the longest established Mercedes truck dealership in the country and one of the top performers. The growth of the company led to the opening of branches in Nottingham and Leicester in 1998, making Mertrux the main Mercedes-Benz dealership in the East Midlands. A fourth site opened in Mansfield in 2004.

Today all four of Don Marshall's children, Ian, Sarah, Judith and Matthew have connections with the business: Ian Marshall is Group Managing Director, Matthew is Group Director/General Manager.

Team development is pursued through the achievement of the nationally recognised Investors in People Award gained in 2001.

With the next generation of Mertrux managers, including Russell Walden Dealer Principal, Les Sadler After Sales Director Designate, Nick Ponting General Van Sales Manager and Ian Brown General Truck Sales Manager, enjoying the same degree of loyalty and support from staff and customers as Don Marshall has had, the company is looking forward to celebrating a very enjoyable Golden Jubilee in 2021, selling and maintaining an ever-more impressive range of Mercedes vehicles to ever-more satisfied customers.

Top: Mercedes-Benz Atego and Axor trucks, with box bodies, supplied in 2007 to Abru Ladders, whose head office is in Belper. Centre: Derby Car Display, pictured in 2006. Below left: The two long bodied, high roofed Mercedes Vito 111 CDI vans supplied by Mertrux alongside Hawk Kawasaki Superbikes. Below: Mertrux sponsored speedway racer, Ben Taylor.

Derby County was formed in 1884 as an off-shoot of Derbyshire County Cricket Club. The name Derby Country FC was settled on after objections from the local football association, who claimed that Derbyshire County FC was too long. Matches were originally played at the Racecourse Ground, the home of the cricket club. In 1895, the club moved to the Baseball Ground where it would remain for 102 years. The first honour the Rams won arrived in 1946 with a 4-1 FA Cup Final defeat of Charlton after extra time. The lack of fortune in the competition up to this point – three final reverses and regular defeats at the semi-final stage – prompted a notion that the club was under the spell of a gypsy curse because of the Baseball Ground being built on a gypsy camping ground. Prior to the 1946 triumph, players even asked gypsies, angry at the development, to lift the curse. These pictures bring back memories of before, during and after the second world war.

Right: Back home in 1972 it was time for the people of Derby to celebrate. Rams players greet thousands of adoring fans who lined the streets in May as the League championship trophy is paraded for the first time in the club's history.

DERBY COUNTY FC

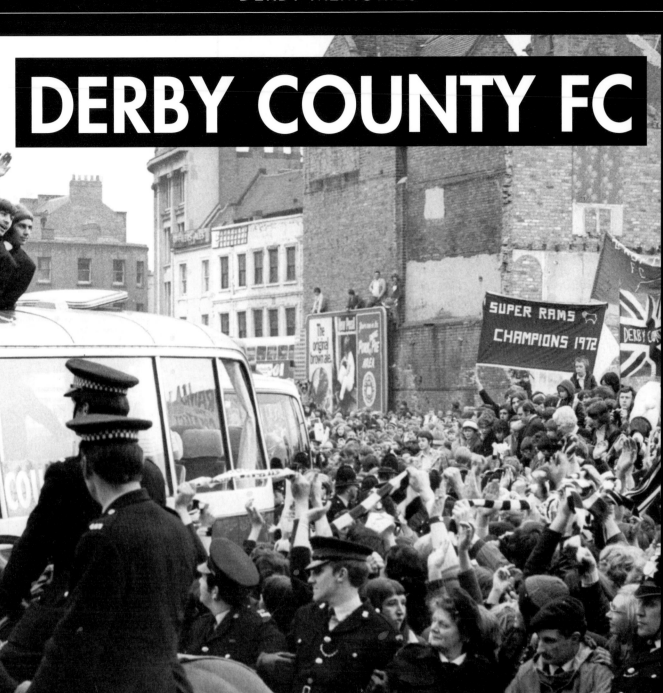

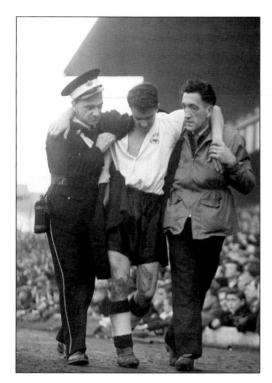

The 1930s were a time for strict discipline at the club, but most professional footballers were all-round sportsmen too and were pictured outside the Markeaton Pavilion in 1934 (bottom left). The same year, the team was asked to tour Germany (far left). The team were asked to give the Nazi salute, but goalkeeper Jack Kirby refused. Four matches were played on a tour, watched by more 100,000 spectators. There were still matches played during the war as the picture below from September 1943 shows, with British soldiers, who were injured on the North African front watching a game at the Baseball Ground. It was injuries of a different kind which saw Jack Parry, left, having to leave the field in a game in March 1953. Parry played 516 games for Derby County and scored 110 goals from 1948-1965. He is shown being carried off the field by an ambulance man and trainer Ralph Hann. Hann was a wing half with the club from 1933-1939 and then trainer from 1953-1967, until Brian Clough brought in his own staff.

It was the proudest moment in Derby County's long footballing history as the team received the FA Cup (right) in 1946 from King George VI. Some 98,000 people packed Wembley Stadium when Derby beat Charlton Athletic 4-1 but only after extra time. The first goal did not come until 80 minutes into the game. Derby scored first but Charlton got an equaliser two minutes later. In extra time one goal from the Rams' Peter Doherty and two from Jackie Stamps sealed the win. Skipper Jack Nicholas was presented with the trophy by the King. Then the jubilant team toured the stadium holding the cup aloft – much to the delight of Rams fans everywhere. It was the first FA Cup success since the club was founded in 1884. Because of travelling restrictions on supporters, teams had competed in a unique two-legged football tournament that year. The railways were run down after the war and it was difficult to travel so in each round of the cup teams played each other home and away. This meant supporters could at least watch the home game. The cup win must have lifted spirits back in Derby where people were starting the long haul back to normality after the second world war. Times were hard and rationing was still in force. But football provided a great escape from the deprivations that dogged life.. Ten minutes before the final whistle Derby went one up thanks to an own goal from Charlton's Bert Turner. But he was responsible for the equaliser two minutes later. His free kick smashed into Peter Doherty's legs before going in. In extra time Derby went ahead courtesy of Doherty and two more goals

from Jackie Stamps sealed the result. The successful Derby County side was: Woodley, Howe, Nicholas, Leuty, Bullions, Harrison Musson, Carter, Doherty Stamps and Duncan. Posing for the formal photograph with the cup back at the Baseball Ground (players only) are: back row, from the left, Jack Parr, who missed the final after breaking his arm, Jim Bullions, Jack Nicholas, Vic Woodley, Jack Howe, Leon Leuty and Chick Musson. Middle row: Sammy Crooks, who was also injured and missed the final, Jack Stamps, Peter Doherty and Raich Carter. On the ground are wingers Reg Harrison and Dally Duncan. Manager Stewart MacMillan is next to Stamps and trainer Dave Willis is extreme right in the middle row.

Derby County had plenty to celebrate in the late 1960s and early 1970s, gaining several league titles.Celebrations are seen in these pictures. Rams skipper Dave Mackay and his team-mates are seen greeting fans on the steps of the Council House in April 1969, after Derby County won the Second Division trophy. Next to Mackay (left with trophy) are Willie Carlin, John McGovern and John Robson. Derby won the title by seven points. Moving on to 1972, there were celebrations at home and abroad. Showing off their musical talents at an impromptu jam session at Calla Millor, Spain, are Jim Walker (guitar), Colin Boulton (drums), Ron Webster (tambourine), Alan Hinton (sax) and John Robson (vocal).

County's greatest success came under Brian Clough, who guided them to the league title in 1972 and the European Cup semi-final against Juventus the following season. The year 1975, saw the Rams claim their second league title under the stewardship of Dave Mackay, who had replaced Clough when he had left the club after falling out with the board. Clough is pictured here (second left) with his assistant Peter Taylor (left), club chairman Sam Longson and Len Shackleton (right) the former Sunderland star who at this time was a journalist based in the North-East and who was the man who recommended them to the Rams. Clough began his football career at his home-town club Middlesbrough, and enjoyed a successful career as a centre-forward with Boro and Sunderland, scoring 204 goals in 222 games and winning two England caps. A knee injury forced him to retire early from playing, but he enjoyed a meteoric rise as a manager. After becoming Hartlepool boss at 30 - then the youngest

manager in the league - Clough moved to Derby, taking them to the Division Two championship and then the Division One title in 1972. He resigned from Derby in 1973 after a conflict with the chairman. He then had brief unsuccessful spells at Brighton and Leeds United before moving to Nottingham Forest in 1975, where he embarked on a hugely successful if unconventional 18-year reign. The League championship and League Cup in 1978 was followed by another League Cup in 1979 and successive European Cup triumphs in 1979 and 1980. He later won Premiership season) ended in relegation for Forest, but his popularity remained undiminished in the East Midlands, and indeed throughout football. He was made a Freeman of Derby in 2003 and died on 20th September, 2004. Peter Taylor was his assistant for many years, spotting players to sign. He later came back on his own in 1982 but could not stop Derby being relegated in 1984. Derby County are pictured with the league championship trophy in this team photograph. Chairman Sam Longson is in the centre with manager Dave Mackay on his left and secretary Stuart

the League Cup two further times with Forest. Only one other British manager won more European Cups - Liverpool boss Bob Paisley. Clough's reputation as a manager was unique. The only major trophy that eluded him in his career was the FA Cup, although what probably disappointed him most was the Football Association's decision not to give him the England job when he was at the peak of his profession. He said the only job that would take him away from Forest would be the England manager's job. Clough remained with Forest until 1993 when he retired - sadly his final campaign (the inaugural Webb on his right. In a photo from a game on 21st April, 1979, Derby players celebrate Gerry Daly's goal against Arsenal at the Baseball Ground. Daly is the player with arms raised. Derby won 2-0. Gerry Daly played for Derby County from 1977 to 1980. Colin Murphy signed him from Manchester United for £175,000 in March 1977. He did not get on with Tommy Docherty, the next Derby manager but later withdrew a transfer request. He won 14 caps for the Republic of Ireland while playing for Derby. He was sold to Coventry City for £310,000. Daly played 122 games for Derby, scoring 34 goals.

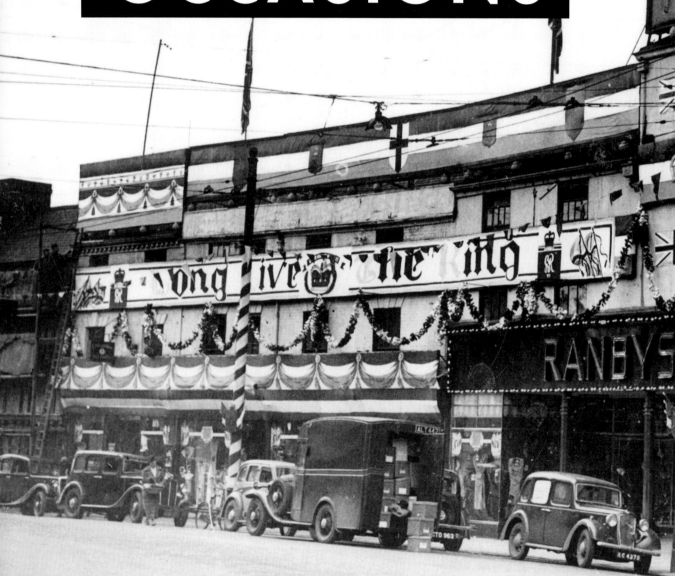

EVENTS & OCCASIONS

The streets were the place to be for the coronation of George VI. This view shows the old Victoria Street frontage of Ranbys department store, which became Debenhams in 1972. It is decorated for the coronation with 'Long Live the King' proudly emblazoned on the front of the store.

over his desire to marry his divorced mistress Wallace Simpson. The day after this picture was taken, he visited Holloway to lay the Foundation Stone of the Florence Nightingale Memorial Hall.

Left: Here Prince Edward is seen walking in close proximity to the crowds (which seems to mainly comprise of adoring women). He is visiting Holloway to lay the Foundation Stone of the Florence Nightingale Memorial Hall. Florence Nightingale was born 1820, the daughter of a Derbyshire landowner and industrialist, revolutionised nursing to become the most famous woman of the millennium.

Top: The location of this photograph is the bottom of Douglas Street. The tramlines can be seen turning off up Douglas St on the left of picture. The area to the right was cleared a few years later to build Ivy Square. The photograph also shows a car transporting a high ranking policemen, who was perhaps part of the official reception committee for the Prince. Prince Edward was at this time Prince of Wales and oldest son of King George V. Within four years of this photograph he would become King Edward VIII, briefly, before abdicating his throne

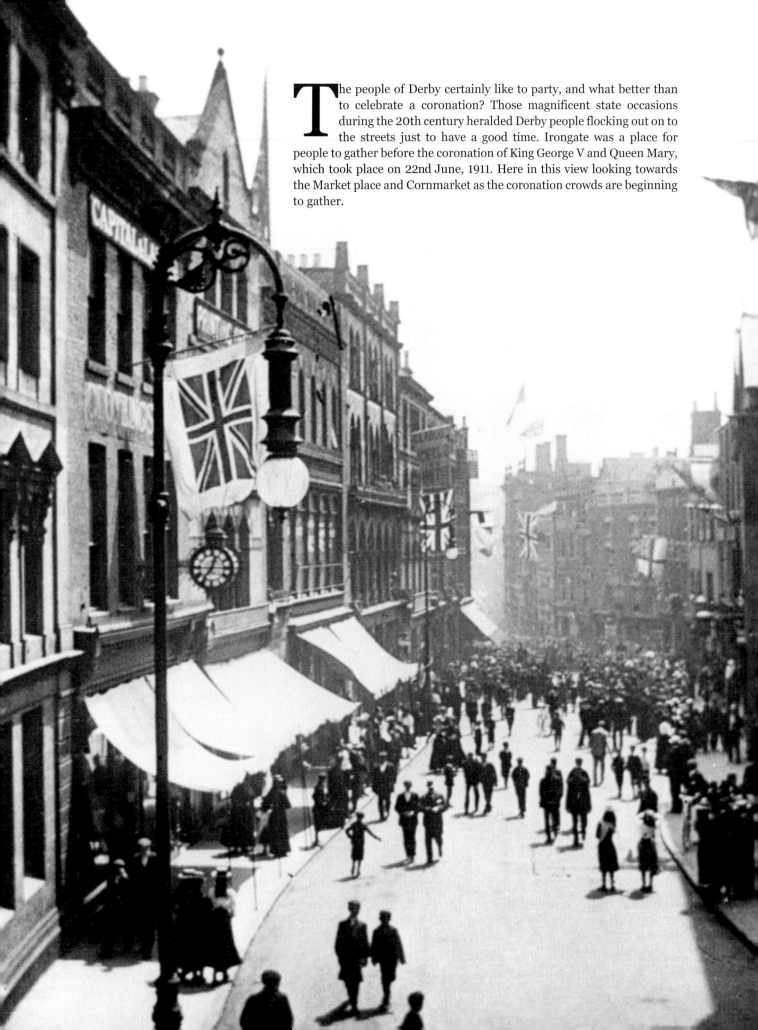

The people of Derby certainly like to party, and what better than to celebrate a coronation? Those magnificent state occasions during the 20th century heralded Derby people flocking out on to the streets just to have a good time. Irongate was a place for people to gather before the coronation of King George V and Queen Mary, which took place on 22nd June, 1911. Here in this view looking towards the Market place and Cornmarket as the coronation crowds are beginning to gather.

Above: The cinema provided the main highlight of social life for many people in the first half of the 20th century. Every small town had its own cinema and Wirksworth was no different. The cinema formed the hub of many people's lives, but this one in Wirksworth closed in 1967. Cinema is coming to life again in the town, with the Wirksworth Film Society. It has already enjoyed five successful years of showing a wide range of first class movies, but at the town hall. As one member commented; "It's been just wonderful being able to walk into town and watch a superb film on the big screen, while sipping a glass of my favourite red wine. Going to one of the big cinemas in the area is such a hassle, and I look forward to seeing what's on offer".Wirksworth has a rich history, which runs from prehistoric times, through the Roman occupation, Saxon and Viking invasions. But a more up to date project is being run by Wirksworth Heritage Centre to collect memories from Wirksworth people of 60 years ago as the second world war came to an end.

Right: The Sunday school treat was something which everyone looked forward to in the first half of the 20th century. It often involved races and picnics with trips to parkland. Processions were important too and enjoyed by all with horsedrawn vehicles parading through the town. The paddock of Derby racecourse, which was off Nottingham Road, to the right of a tree-lined avenue, was one popular venue for the Sunday School Treat after children had been pulled round

the streets on decorated drays. The treat pictured took place on 6th June, 1922 and is seen parading through the streets of Little Chester (Chester Green). This is the most historic area of Derby, the location of a large fortified Roman settlement, which they called Derventio. This fort, which later became a town, not only protected the river crossing, but also stood at the junction and gave protection to five Roman roads. The most important was Ryknield Street which connected Gloucester and the West Country with Yorkshire and the North East. Little of the Roman settlement remains at Little Chester today, apart from two Roman wells, one on Marcus Street and the other in the garden of the vicarage of St Paul's Church. However, a series of excavations in the last 50 years have established both its importance and prosperity, including the discovery of an underfloor heating system and an abundance of coins. The district has been continually inhabited since the departure of the Romans, next being settled by the Saxons. Chester Green, the open land which is the centrepiece of the area, is first referred to by name in written records dating back to 1495 and has been a public park since 1866. In modern times the name Chester Green, applied to the district as a whole, seems to have overtaken the "correct" name in popular usage.

Above: The Mayor and Mayoress of Derby opening the Mickleover Boy's Club in August 1942. The Boy's Club was on the site of the ex-Methodist Chapel in Orchid Street just off the Market Place. The Club would later become Mickleover Boy's FC in the Derby Senior league and have more recently become Mickleover Sports. The team now play in the Northern Counties Football League Premier Division.

Below: The present factory was established in 1878, however the business can trace its origins to the factory on Nottingham Road some time before 1750. The opening of a London Showroom in 1773 marked the beginning of the widespread recognition of the excellence of Derby porcelain. King George III, recognising the uniqueness of Derby porcelain, when he granted the factory the rare honour of being able to incorporate a crown into the backstamp in 1775. Much later, in 1890, Queen Victoria also gave Crown Derby her seal of approval not only by awarding the royal warrant, but also by granting the title 'The Royal Crown Derby Porcelain Company'. After his father's death in 1786, William Duesbury II set about making the Derby China Works the finest in Europe. Great developments were made in body, glaze, potting and decoration and the factory benefited from a highly talented group of ceramic artists, including Boreman, the water-colour landscape genius; figure painters Askew and Banford; and the exceptional talents of flower painters Withers, Billingsley and Pegg. A tremendous variety of objects has made the 1786-95 decade one of the most desirable and interesting for collectors and students

alike. When William Duesbury died in 1797 at the early age of 34, many of his remarkable team left the factory which led to a temporary decline in the fortunes of Crown Derby. It was Robert Bloor who restored the Derby porcelain reputation when he took control of the factory in 1811 and began to build a team of very fine painters. Many rich and elegant services were produced at this time and shapes tended to be larger and more flamboyant. Typical of the period are the lavishly decorated Japan, or Imari, patterns which are still very popular today. Confidence in the Crown Derby name was underwritten in 1877 by the opening of an impressive new factory at Osmaston Road, Derby. This was the beginning of a period of growth and diversification which has continued to the present day. Royal acclaim followed in 1890 when the company was appointed 'Manufacturers of porcelain to Her Majesty'. Royal Crown Derby was acquired by S Pearson and Son, the Pearson family company, to become part of their Allied English Potteries group. Brian Branscombe was appointed Art Director, and established the new graphic and printing departments. Pearson subsequently bought Royal Doulton. The company was then merged into the larger group. In 2000, when Royal Crown Derby celebrated 250 years of porcelain manufacture in Derby, Hugh Gibson, a former director of Royal Doulton and member of the Pearson family, led a buy-out of Royal Crown Derby, making the firm an independent and privately owned concern.

Above: Royal visits to the Derby have been numerous over the years and 1936 was no exception, even though it was the year King George V died. That year, as the guest of Sir William and Noreen Bass, the Princess Royal attended Derby Races in November. The same month, the Duke and Duchess of Gloucester were guests of Sir Ian Walker at Osmaston Manor, for pheasant shooting. The Duchess had been in Derby the previous month when she laid the foundation stone of the £100,000 extension to Derbyshire Royal Infirmary. Here she is pictured walking through a guard of honour made up of the hospital's nursing staff. The DRI is a commonly-used abbreviation for the hospital, originally began life in 1810 on land formerly part of the Castlefields estate. The hospital was rebuilt in 1891 and Queen Victoria laid the foundation stone on May 21. The Duke of Devonshire unveiled the statue of Florence Nightingale at the DRI, on the June 12, 1914.

Left: The flags, either side of the trolley bus wires, are out in St Peter's Street on this fine day to welcome Princess Elizabeth to Derby. Three years later as Queen Elizabeth II she would be opening Parliament: on this day in 1949 however the heir to the throne, unsuspecting of the awesome responsibilitieis which would have to assume all too soon, had come to Derby to open the Council House. With war now in the past women were dressing up again as witnessed by the two young ladies crossing the road. In the war years clothing became scarce as manufacturers in Britain had more important items to make for the war effort. The war made the import of cloth and other materials from abroad almost impossible. Clothes rationing had begun on the 1st June 1941 with clothing ration coupon books being issued to every man, woman and child. Each person was allowed coupons equivalent to one complete outfit per year. A total of 66 coupons were allowed per year for an adult, and children half that amount.

Left: While today's National Health Service may have much publicised money problems the situation was much different and perhaps worse during the first half of the 20th century. Then hospitals had to depend on private subscription and were always in need of money. Hospital Sunday became an annual event, when a large procession paraded through the town to join with hundreds of assembled people. The purpose was to raise money for local hospitals. This picture from 1935 shows part of the procession, which wound its way through the town to Markeaton Park. These parades ceased with the formation of the NHS in 1948. The picture shows the float of the Trent Motor Traction Company. It was formed in October 1913 in a joint venture, which involved BET, under whose influence Trent was to remain until NBC control in 1969. Serving the area around its watery namesake, Trent was involved in both coach and bus operations and helped in the establishment of revolutionary new vehicles. It built up an intensive network of services based on Derby, for which it had one of the most interesting fleets of buses and coaches, including for many years vehicles manufactured by the Midland Red company.

Left: Royal visits are not a rare thing in Derby and Prince Charles has been to the city several times. In this picture he is seen being presented to the Bishop of Derby in Derby Cathedral in November 1979. It was to be a more momentous occasion on his next visit about 16 months later because it was a few days after his engagement to Lady Diana Spencer that Prince Charles made an eventful return to the city. Then, he promised the residents who handed over congratulation cards and engagement presents that she would be with him on his next visit to the city. The visit was scheduled for five hours - but lasted well over six, with the Prince even skipping his lunch break so he could cram in as much as possible.

Below: On 28th July, 1977, Derby became a city. It was extra special as it was the year of the Queen's Silver Jubilee. It also meant a royal visit and the Queen came to confer city status on the town of Derby. Adoring crowds greeted the monarch as she made her way to the Council House for the ceremony. The event took place just a month after the town had celebrated the Silver Jubilee. Many people remember lining the streets as the Queen toured the country's newest city or holding street parties to celebrate. Derby was awarded the honour in recognition for its achievements over the years and for its heritage as an industrial nerve centre. This view is looking along Irongate towards All Saints' Church. It was built as a minster church in around the year 925, with the tower added later in 1511-32. The church, the majority of which was rebuilt in 1723 by James Gibbs, became a cathedral in 1927. This picture from the silver jubilee year shows Irongate decorated with bunting for the royal visit. It shows the cathedral at the top and Irongate Furnishing Stores, W. Robinson and the Irongate Tavern on the right.

The Queen's visit was not the only Royal visit to Derby in 1977. On 9th November, the Queen Mother attended the opening night of the new Assembly Rooms, where she watched the Royal Philharmonic Orchestra try out the acoustics of Derby's newest entertainment venue. It was the second Royal visit within six months - the Queen had visited the city in July on her Jubilee tour of Britain and bestowed city status on Derby. The Queen Mother, then 77, arrived to cheering crowds on a brisk November morning and was greeted by, among others, the city's mayor at the time, Councillor Jeffrey Tillett. While in the city she also visited St Christopher's Orphanage. It had formerly been called the Railway Servants Orphanage. The building was constructed by A A Langley, the Midland Railway Architect in 1887. It closed in 1980. The second picture shows the mayor welcoming the Queen Mother to the Assembly Rooms. He said: "I had to take her on a tour of the building and we miscalculated the speed at which she would move. "She had tremendous energy and we were several minutes ahead of schedule. "Fortunately, she stopped to have a chat with the ladies behind the bar and we were soon back on course." Following the tour of the new building, The Queen Mother watched an opening night concert by the Royal Philharmonic Orchestra, of which she was Patron. Tickets for that first concert were £1.50, £2.50 and £3.50. Concert proceeds of £1,000 were sent to the Queen's Jubilee Appeal.

The Queen Mother brought a touch of West End glamour to the city when she arrived swathed in diamonds, pearls and a white mink stole. Derby's original Assembly Rooms building was built between 1752 and 1755.The building was gutted by fire in 1963. The five bay stone facade to the building was re-erected at Crich Tramway Village, home of the National Tramway Museum, where it still stands. Between 1973 and 1977 work was carried out on a replacement Assembly Rooms. The long section of the building was once the north west side of the Market Place, which formerly housed a row of Georgian and Victorian shops.The Tourist Information Centre now stands on the site of the original Assembly Rooms.

Above: Just a small part of the adoring crowds who turned to greet the Queen when she arrived in Derby to confer its city status on 28th July, 1977. The event coincided with the Queen's Silver Jubilee so there was dual cause for celebration and the people of Derby turned out in force. Crowds began to gather at the railway station and in total around 60,000 people, queueing 10-deep in places, lined the streets in the early hours waiting for the royal couple. Led by the regimental band of the Worcestershire and Sherwood Foresters the royal couple were driven along a processional route to the Council House, where Mayor of Derby Councillor Jeffery Tillett conducted them up the stairs to the balcony, so that they could wave to the crowds. After the official ceremony, the royal couple went on a walkabout round Derby Market Place, where the band of the 9th/12th Royal Lancers helped create a carnival atmosphere. From there, the Queen diverted from her planned route to call at The Leylands, of which she had become patron since her previous visit to Derby in 1957. Just seven minutes late, she arrived at Butterley Hall to officially open Derbyshire Police Headquarters and chat to the 10,000-strong crowd who had been waiting patiently to greet her.

The Queen arrived by train at 10am and was welcomed by the Lord Lieutenant of Derbyshire, Sir Ian Walker-Okeover. Also waiting on the platform were British Rail employees and 18 Brownies from Nottingham. When the first of many unofficial floral gifts was handed over by two young sisters, the Queen apparently asked: "Have you picked these flowers out of your garden?"Adoring crowds lined the street to greet the monarch as she made her way to the Council House for the ceremony. Derby was awarded the honour in recognition for its achievements over the years, for its heritage as an industrial nerve centre. Thousands of people took to the streets hoping for a glimpse of the Queen as she made her way through the city centre to perform the ceremony. Some people got a close-up view, like the jubilant crowds who greeted her as she left the Midland Railway Station. There were more flag waving Royal fans as the Queen went by the Assembly Rooms and then before the ceremony she had time to stop and talk to senior citizens in wheelchairs who had gathered in Corporation Street to wish her well.

SHOPPING SPREE

East Street is and was a busy place for shoppers. This picture from the 1940s shows two of its most well known stores, the Midland Drapery on the left and Boots on the right. The Midland Drapery building was built in 1882 and demolished in 1970. Edwin Ann established the Midland Drapery on St Peter's Street and the East Street development was added in 1892. As well as St Peter's Street, the shop occupied numbers 1-9 East Street,

number 3 being the men's wear department, stocking hosiery, pants, vests, shirts in wool, collars and cuffs, ties, caps, rugs and umbrellas. During the late 19th and early 20th century the Midland Drapery was one of the largest department stores in the country. In 1909 it employed 300 people, many of whom appeared to have enjoyed working for Edwin Ann as he was regarded as a considerate employer, organising company events to such destinations as Chatsworth including all hospitality and entertainment.

After the demolition, the Eagle Centre Market was built with an entrance on East Street. The centre occupied a 12 acre site between St Peter's Street, London Road and Morledge. The indoor market replaced the old outdoor market on Morledge, next to the bus station. It was extensively rebuilt in the early 1990s. The exterior of the Boots store was described as an ornate neo-jacobean-tudoresque façade. It was built in 1938. The building is currently occupied by the Halifax Bank.

Above: By the look of the people of Derby in this picture of St Peter's Bridge taken at the lower end of St Peter's Street it is evident that people are in step with the fast moving times. Events in this year of 1948 outside the town would affect every one of these people, and everyone who has been to see the doctor, for this was the year Health Minister Aneurin Bevan announced the introduction of the National Health Service - and over 47 million Britons were treated in the first 12 months. Air freight transport rose to new heights with the Russians blockading Berlin, and we and the Americans broke the blockade by air lifting enough food to feed and warm the Berliners for over a year. The end of food and clothing purchase restrictions after the war changed our daily lives whilst Burtons the Tailors on each side of the road were changing the way we looked with non-utility clothing, and with all the changes came prosperity for the survivors: those who came back from the armed forces and those to whom they returned. All those who had contributed in one way or another to the victory had money to spend, and here they are, taking it out of the Midland Bank on the left by the traffic signals, and spending it on fine clothes, over the road at Marks and Spencers.

Right: This was the age of the 'New Look' in fashion when hemlines, which had been just above the knee to save material, took the country by storm and clothes rationing was finished. Could that be Charlie crossing the road to get a bottle of wine. That looks like Bert and Elsie heading for some butter and eggs from the Maypole. Fiona and Gareth hadn't even been thought of. Some of the pedestrians in the picture could have been amongst the 8,000 Londoners who had come to Derby to escape the pilotless German V1/V2 flying bombs, and stayed after the war. Maybe you're even one of them, and remember those buzz bombs and the heart stopping times spent waiting from when you heard the motor stop, until it hit someone's home, leaving people helpless on the ground. Nothing ever stands still. This 1948 picture shows H Samuels the jewellers, before it went on the move, taking its well known clock to the junction with Albert Street, and from Ramsdens restaurant it all changed in about 1968 for renovated and rebuilt premises such as Littlewoods store. Two years preceding the scene before your eyes, the Derby Rotary Club decided to promote the foundation of a War Memorial Village for disabled servicemen at a cost of £100,000, with the project to be run by a co-operative of twenty four. The opening stages were celebrated when on 27th June, 1949 the then Princess Elizabeth came and gave it the Royal seal of approval. By 1972 there were 38 homes, which later were absorbed into the community.

positioned to carry the power for the trolley bus network. Beneath them the sign indicating the routes to Uttoxeter, Ashbourne and Manchester can be seen, fixed to one of the tall poles attached to the trolley cables. It is difficult to appreciate that the congestion caused to the centre of towns and cities like Derby before the 1960s occurred as a result of 'through' traffic destined for far flung destinations having to squeeze through the centre of most of the towns along the way. The age of motorways and inner relief roads would change all that from the 1960s onwards, making our town

Top right: This crowded Derby shopping scene is capable of rekindling memories among those with a love of the city. The picture is dominated by the tangle of electricity cables and city centres cleaner, healthier and safer. This view of St. Peter's Street shows Maypole Dairies and H. Samuel's businesses across the street from the camera.

Left: Boots the chemist had simple origins not very away from Derby and then grew into the major national chain it is today. This picture of the window of one of its Derby shops highlights a spring cleaning promotion within the store and appears to have been taken in the 1960s. As well as many of Boots own brand products on show, there are well known names such as Handy Andy and 1001 and all the prices are still in pounds, shillings and pence as decimalisation did not take place until 1971. The company's founder John Boot was born in Radcliffe-on-Trent in 1815 and his early life was spent as an agricultural labourer on local farms. It was a poor area and Boot became involved in chapel affairs and local schemes to improve living conditions. Herbal remedies were popular with the labouring poor, who could not afford the services of a physician. His mother had used herbs for healing and he may also have been familiar with remedies published by John Wesley. In 1849, with the assistance of his father-in-law and the support of the local Methodist community, John opened The British and American Botanic Establishment at 6 Goose Gate, Nottingham, hoping to provide physical comfort to the needy, as well as a reasonable living for his family. John and his wife, Mary, prepared many remedies themselves. However he died in 1860, at the age of 45. Mary took over management of the shop, with the help of her 10-year-old son, Jesse, who gathered and prepared herbs as well as serving behind the counter. It was Jesse who later started the build-up and rapid expansion of the company. In 1877 Jesse took sole control of the shop and with takings of £100 a week, he became one of the busiest shopkeepers and the largest dealer in patent medicines in Nottingham. The company prospered and he soon acquired other premises in Nottingham before spreading further afield. For 13 years the company was owned by an American group, although with Jesse's son John playing a leading role. With the US depression, Boots was sold back to a group of British financiers with John as chairman and managing director. Boots continued to grow. Alliance Boots was formed on 31st July, 2006 through the merger of Alliance UniChem Plc and Boots Group PLC. On 26th June, 2007 the company was acquired by AB Acquisitions Limited.

Right: This display gave a prominent showing to soaps and washing powders from the Co-operative Wholesale Society. It was part of a window display competition held in 1928 by the National Co-operative Propaganda Campaign. There is nothing to indicate whether this particular display won a prize, but it was certainly impressive with trade names such as Solvo, Microl and Minerva. The CWS had manufactured soap since 1875, soap powders from the turn of the century and flakes from 1915. The trend away from producer co-operatives such as the Rochdale Pioneers, which was formed in the early 1840s, was accelerated by the evolution of the Co-operative Wholesale Society and its growing influence in formulating co-operative policy. The initial attempt to begin a wholesale society in Rochdale had ended in partial failure, but when the society was re-established in Manchester, in 1864, it enjoyed immediate and spectacular success. As the CWS expanded, it became obvious that it was a thriving profit-making organisation and many of the older members of the Co-operative movement became increasingly unhappy at the spectacle of co-operative organisations employing huge numbers of workers who had no control or share in the management of the ventures. They had always envisaged co-operation as a movement of both producers and consumers, not as merely another capitalist employer. On the other hand, there was an equally vociferous body of opinion, which regarded co-operation as a consumer society providing wholesale, unadulterated food at reasonable prices with the added incentive of the "divi". Eventually J T W Mitchell became chairman of the wholesale society in 1874. He stood firm on his commitment (made during his period with the Co-operative Manufacturing Society) to co-operation as a consumer-orientated movement. Under his leadership, British co-operation became consciously the predominantly consumers' movement it has remained ever since.

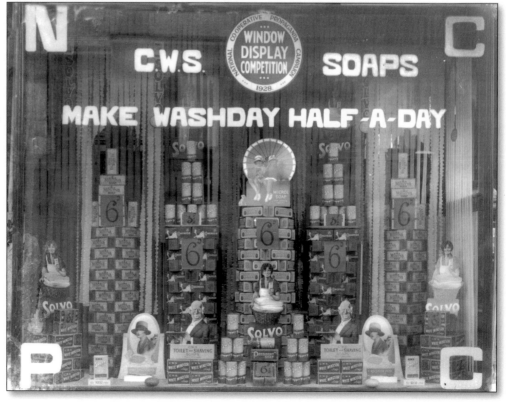

Above: Derby's impressive Market Hall was built in the 1860s at a cost of £29,000. It was opened to the public in 1866. The foundation stone was laid on 16th February, 1864, by the Mayor. In 1989 the Market Hall was restored and opened by Princess Margaret on 27th November that year. This photograph goes back to the Market Hall of the 1920s and shows stallholders, staff and customers at a shop selling newspapers. It is likely, but not certain, that it is that of the current market's oldest stall,

Poynton's the newsagents, which has been delivering the news to Derby people for almost 160 years. The dynasty began when Irishman Patrick Poynton opened a newsagent's shop in Brook Street, in 1848. Twenty years later, when the new Market Hall opened alongside Derby Market Place, he decided to spread his wings and open a stall there. The borough architect and surveyor designed the covered Market Hall in 1864. It had a spectacular vaulted roof using iron from a nearby foundry. The Market Hall opened for business on 29th May, 1866, when it was given a rousing welcome with a gala concert and a choir who sang the Messiah. Today, gathered there, six days a week, in the Grade II listed building, are no less than 70 stalls specialising in all sorts of trades, ranging from the trendy to the traditional.

Below: You are on Victoria Street, looking up Green Lane with Ranby's store now Debenham's on the right. At the other side is Woolworths, which opened its doors in 1911. In those days it was themed on the American five and ten cent store, and advertised that no single item cost more than sixpence. Next to Woolworths was Jeromes, the while-you-wait portrait photographers, in case you needed a passport picture for your trip on the Titanic, just launched down its Belfast slipway. On the corner with Green Lane was Meesons Ltd, and the area where the lorry and van are coming out of Green Lane has since been paved over.

The Market Place looks a lot different today to what it looked when this picture was taken looking from Irongate in 1908. Trams and market stalls were the main attraction then. The most recent addition to today's Market Place is the ice rink in place over the winter period. Every third Thursday of athe month, the large open area of the Market Place is enlivened by Farmers' Market stalls selling locally grown and sourced produce. Excavations have revealed that the Market Place almost certainly did not come into existence until around 1100. An ancient trackway that bisected the town ran along the south side of the Market Place. Rapid expansion took place after the Norman Conquest and other markets sprang up. In the Corn Market grain was traded, at the top end of Friar Gate farm animals were bought and sold along with produce. A market was also developed in the Morledge, where fairs were held. Behind the stalls can be seen the Guildhall and next to it the offices of the Derbyshire Advertiser. The Hobson family were founders, proprietors and editors of the Derbyshire Advertiser throughout its long existence - but they also produced a Mayor of Derby, two leading economists, two academics and a chairman of a nationalised industry. The family goes back to Robert Hobson (1752-1821), although it was his son, John, who laid the foundations for the family's success. He set up in Ashbourne as a currier in the leather trade, before becoming a bookseller, publisher, author, auctioneer and valuer. He founded the Advertiser. Hobsons remained as editors until Charles Mortimer Hobson (1892-1964) retired in 1953, handing over to the E. G. Barry Atkinson, his cousin by marriage. The paper closed on his retirement - its fifth and final editor-proprietor - in 1969. The Derbyshire Advertiser opened its first Derby offices in the Market Place around 1855, but in 1862, the ancient Cross Keys Inn was advertised to let, and William Hobson acquired the lease and closed the pub, refurbishing the building as the newspaper's head office. Pre-dating Harold Lloyd's celluloid stunts on the silent screen by a few years, the workman on the top right of the photograph, perched high above the street, is taking his life in his hands. No elf'n'safety legislation in those days!

Right: This is the lower part of St Peter's Street with the Midland Drapery on the right, a Company founded by Edwin Thomas Ann. A Welshman by birth in 1852 he came to open his store in Derby in 1882 in St Peter's Street. His business prospered and he expanded it into what was Bag Lane which was renamed East Street in the time of Queen Victoria. He was liked by those who knew him and respected by all. In due course he became an Alderman, and a Justice of the Peace. He was the Mayor of Derby in 1898-1899. and again in 1905-1906, and was knighted by King Edward VII in 1906. His ways were always courtly, and he greeted those who worked for him each day with a smile and a friendly word. When he died in 1913 the streets through which his funeral cortege travelled were lined with Derbeians, paying their respects as to a real friend and benefactor, for he gave many gifts to the town, not least of which was an ambulance. His emporium grew in four stages and was identified instantly by the image of a very large magnet, which did succeed in drawing the customers. When all the building was finished it had a frontage of 115 yards along St Peters and East Streets. For the ladies who worked at the store who lived out of town there was in-store accommodation, and the men stayed at a London Road hostel. The store closed in the 1970s.

Below: Taking another walk along St Peter Street, the eroded pavements tell their own story of an affluent society with every kind of road transport from bus to Rolls Royce, from van to wagon, sports car to saloon, motor-bike to pedal bike, to foot power. On the right, one of Derby's most famous stores up to July 1970, a store which was the equal of any London department store in range and quality of products. It was the enterprise of two men, Harry Thurman and William Malin, who were both employed at George and George, the woollen and silk specialists. When G and G closed in mid 1870s Thurman and Malin crossed St Peter's Street and set up their business in the imposing four storey premises which featured a frontage decorated with bronze which was always highly polished. Business was rewarding at numbers 8 and 9 and their frontage grew into St Peter's church yard. The electric lift installed to all sales floors was an innovation which provided the right image of superior customer service, and in 1929 Thurman and Malins' store was celebrating with a grand golden jubilee sale which generated enormous sales.

Left: St Peter's Street looking towards The Spot. Taken in 1948, this shows why the dramatic changes which have taken place were necessary, for here is a town of narrow street by today's requirements, crowded to distraction within the confines of its road frame. The Wolsley is still with us at this time, an elegant car and one that felt rather like a bus to drive, easier when they had power steering. The trolley, which is serving a community out at Allestree, has suburbanised the village to Derby and changed their pattern of shopping. The post-war baby boom (over 20% higher than needed to maintain the status quo), the National Health Service that looks after you from cradle to grave, the comprehensive school based on ensuring equal opportunity for all; all this added up to this scenario and the need for action. 'The wind of change,' as someone said,'is blowing and it is easier to go with it than not.' Appropriately enough someone else said, 'If you don't want to come, get off the bus.' Very few ever do.

Right: Cornmarket always has been a thriving city centre street, which was eventually pedestrianised in the 1990s. This picture, taken in the early 1960s, looks north towards the Market Place. At the far end of the row nearest Market Place is the Kardomah Cafe. The ground floor of Devonshire House contains the shops of Spalls and T Smithard's hams and bacon shop. On the right is H Samuel, with its famous clock.

Bottom left: This view of a bus travelling along St James' Street in this picture taken in 1970, is unlikely to be seen again, for the street closed to traffic and was pedestrianised in the 1990s. Not only does this picture show Barclays Bank on the right, but also one of the shops of Birds the Confectioners. The bakery was founded by three brothers, Frank, Thomas and Reginald Bird in 1919. They had returned from fighting in the first world war. The company was carried on by the sons of Thomas and Reginald Bird when their fathers died in the mid 1930s. Frank Bird died in 1951. The company is currently under the management of the third generation. Birds now operates 49 shops around the East Midlands. The latest shop to be added to the company was the Expresso in the Eagle Centre. Each shop is delivered fresh goods daily. All of Birds' produce is manufactured at one bakery on Ascot Drive, Derby. Birds runs a "Made fresh daily" policy, with "We never sell a stale cake" printed on every cake box and bag. St James' Street came about after the Markeaton Brook, which had previously run openly along Brookside, was culverted. St James' Lane, little more than an alleyway, was widened and paid

for by the building of the St James' Hotel (on the left). It was renamed St James' Street and became an elegant shopping thoroughfare.

Above: Sadler Gate was pedestrianised in the early 1970s and links the Market Place and Irongate with Bold Lane and The Strand. It is now the fashionable place to be seen and to shop, with many avant-garde shops, clubs and eating houses. It's a hive of activity during the day with the emphasis on shopping and eating. Evening time sees a transformation when the clubs, bars and pubs attract crowds of fun seekers and diners. Sadler Gate was originally home to more mundane, yet essential businesses like that run by the Keeling family, who were labourers and silk weavers, and their neighbour, John Halbord, a bell hanger whose services would have been vital to all the parish churches in the town. In the mid 1800s Sadler Gate would have been a chaotic mix of people making barrels, creating pots and baking breads. Here, too, were charwomen, cork cutters and cordwainers, who traditionally fashioned leather and were, by the 19th century, largely upmarket shoemakers. Visible on the left of the picture is the Old Bell Hotel, one of the oldest coaching inns in Derby, which has managed to retain much of its original appearance, although its apparent Tudor timbering was not added until after the First World War. It is reputed to be haunted by several ghosts. The building on the right corner is Lloyds TSB. It was once the home of William Bemrose (1792-1880) of Bemrose Stationers and printers. He set up business here in 1827 where he pioneered new techniques in lithography and colour printing. His son Henry Howe Bemrose (1827-1911) became Mayor of Derby in 1877.

Above: The people in the picture provide a more typical view of the way St James' Street looks today, as the street closed to traffic and was pedestrianised in the 1990s. St James' Lane, as it was originally known first came into being around 1250. It was little more than an alleyway, but once it was widened and renamed St James' Street it became an elegant shopping thoroughfare. The quality of the architecture with its wonderful four-story Victorian masterpieces can clearly be seen in this picture taken in 1970, showing Barclays Bank and Birds the confectioners. At the time St James' Street was still a busy thoroughfare for traffic, but the number of pedestrians about indicates a foretaste of what was to come after vehicles were banished from the area.

Right: The historic Irongate was a busy place back in 1974 when this picture was taken. There was plenty of traffic, both vehicular and pedestrian and even lots of room to park. Among those parked on the right of the picture, looking from the junction with Saldergate is a Morris Minor Traveller – an iconic car of its time with its unique wooden frame. Money also was a feature, in different ways, with a place to keep your money on the left – Lloyds Bank – and a place to lose it on the right – Ladbrokes. The view is along Irongate with its Joseph Wright memorial. Wright, a genre and portrait painter, was born at 32, Irongate in 1734. He remained in Derby for most of his life, until his death in 1797. He is best known for his industrial scenes such as "The Air Pump" (1768, Tate, London), and his treatment of artificial light. The focus travels along Irongate towards All Saints' Cathedral. The cathedral, once All Saints' Parish Church, now mainly dates to the 18th century (but with a 16th century tower) and was granted cathedral status in 1927.

SPECIAL CAR

19

TRANSPORT

SPECIAL CAR

TRY LEDGERS Tailoring ST PETER'S STREET. 1/2 NOTTINGHAM DAILY EXPRESS THE MORNING PAPER FOR DERBY.

DERBY

Derby Corporation electric trams nos. 19 and 7 stand at the Vicarage Avenue terminus on the first day of services over the route along Burton Road. The Mayor, Alderman Cornelius Boam is in the centre, while F Harding, manager of the tramway undertaking, stands fourth from left. Vicarage Avenue was the original terminus of the Burton Road route; it was extended to a point just beyond Whitaker Road in 1908. The trams along Burton Road were replaced by trolleybuses in 1932.

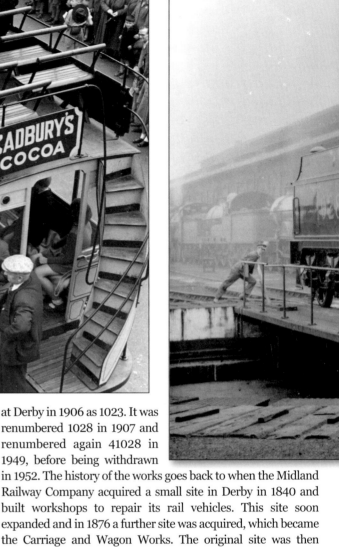

Above: All kinds of massive events were planned to celebrate Derby's octo-centenary. They involved parades and ceremonial events including the Mayor of Derby touring the indoor and outdoor markets and the cattle market. There was also a football match between Derby Boys and Leicester Boys at the Baseball Ground and a banquet at Markeaton. There was a parade through the streets led by the mayor riding in a vintage Rolls Royce culminating in a carnival at Markeaton Park. This replica Derby Tramways Company horse bus was used in the parade through the street as part of the 1954 celebrations. This picture, with crowds lining the pavements, is believed to have been taken in Albert Street. It was in 1154 that Derby was first given a charter (a document granting the townspeople certain rights). In 1204 a new charter gave the people of Derby the right to rule themselves. They were allowed to elect two bailiffs who ran the town. The merchants of Derby were also allowed to form a merchant's guild. The guild regulated trade in the town and protected its member's interests. The name Derby itself is believed to come from deoraby, a word used by the Danes for a deer village, or a village with a deer park.

Top right: This looks like hard work for the two men turning this railway engine round on the turntable at the former Derby Locomotive Works. The site, part of which now houses Pride Park, originally had vast array of engineering skills grouped together to produce what were arguably some of the finest railway locomotives this country has seen. The engine, pictured here outside No 4 shed in the 1930s, is a 4-4-0 locomotive built at Derby in 1906 as 1023. It was renumbered 1028 in 1907 and renumbered again 41028 in 1949, before being withdrawn in 1952. The history of the works goes back to when the Midland Railway Company acquired a small site in Derby in 1840 and built workshops to repair its rail vehicles. This site soon expanded and in 1876 a further site was acquired, which became the Carriage and Wagon Works. The original site was then devoted to the building and repair of locomotives and became Derby Locomotive Works. In 1923 the it came under the control of the London Midland and Scottish Railway (LMS) and in 1948 the British Transport Commission Workshops Division. In 1970 British Rail Engineering Limited (BREL) was formed taking in all British Railways workshops this was one of the country's largest engineering concerns. Before privatisation BREL announced nearly 1,500 redundancies in 1987. GEC bid for the company but the then Transport Secretary decreed that a consortium made up of property giant Trafalgar House, ASEI Brown-Boveri (ABB) and the management (and employees) of BREL were the preferred bidders. The evening newspaper of 7th December, 1990 announced on the front page "BREL shuts Loco Works" and reported on a gradual closure over the next two years. Ultimately only the former 9 and 7 shops remained firstly controlled by AdTranz (a merger of ABB and Mercedes Benz) and finally Bombardier Transportation, while some of the original buildings including the historic round shed are preserved. On 17th March, 2004 Bombardier Transportation

announced Europe-wide redundancies owing to poor performance where profit is concerned.

Below: The old Derby Corporation buses were an everyday sight throughout the city and fondly remembered by transport enthusiasts. There was no shortage of buses in the centre of the city as this picture taken in Corporation Street during the 1960s clearly demonstrates. In between the clock tower of the Guildhall on the left and the cathedral tower, said to be the second highest in England at 212 feet with the oldest peal of 10 bells in the world, seen on the right, several buses can be spotted moving along the street. In 1924 Derby Corporation began operating local buses in Derby. Daimler was the main provider of vehicles at this time. The buses carried a green and cream livery. The bus featured in the centre had a route 27 number with the bus station as its destination. This Derby Corporation bus No.140 (YRC 140), was a 1962 Daimler CVG6 with a Roe body. It was withdrawn in 1974 and sold to Johnson of Worksop for scrap in 1976. On 26th October, 1986, Derby City Transport became an "arm's-length" limited company, Derby City Transport Limited, under the terms of the new Transport Act. This effectively took the Transport Department out of the municipal sector, although the company's major shareholder continued to be the council until 1994, when the undertaking passed to the British Bus organisation, finally ending municipal involvement in Derby's transport system after more than 80 years.

Right: This picture taken in Victoria Street on 2nd July, 1934 shows the end of one era and the start of another. It shows Derby Corporation electric tram No 78 waiting to return to the Abingdon Street car sheds from Victoria Street on the official last run of a Derby tram, the final public services of workmen's trips between Victoria Street and Nightingale Road had ceased two days earlier. On the right of the picture is one of the replacement trolleybuses (No. 127) working service 22 from Ashbourne Road to the Midland Station. Tram No 78 had been built by Brush as recently as 1927 and lasted just seven years before being scrapped. Trolleybus No 127 was a Guy BTX vehicle, new in March 1934. It was withdrawn in 1949. Electric trams had become a regular feature in Derby by 1907 as these "state-of-the-art" tramcars took over from horse-drawn vehicles. The process had started on Wednesday 27th July, 1904, when electric services had commenced on the first routes to the Midland Station, Alvaston and Osmaston Road.

But it was in June 1907 when Derby said goodbye to the corporation horse trams which had plied the town streets for 27 years. Initially run by the Derby Tramways Company, the service was taken over by the corporation in 1899. The era of the electric tram ended in 1934 and the era of the trolleybus began. The trolleybuses ran throughout the city until 1967, before giving way to diesel-powered buses.

Left: Derby inhabitants flocked to the Market Place on this day in January 1932 to see a new form of transport designed to replace the city's trams. It was the first public appearance of a trolley bus in the city as Derby Corporation No.84 (RC 406, but running on trade plates 120 CH) underwent tests. The "No.34 Special" was a Guy BTX with Brush bodywork, and remained in service until 1946. A total of 23 trolley buses were bought in the first half of 1932, the first route commissioned being from the Market Place to Nottingham Road Creamery (now known as Raynesway) on 9th January. By 1934 trolley buses had replaced all of Derby's electric trams, the first line to go being the Nottingham Road route, which was abandoned in November 1930. The trolley buses ruled the roost throughout Derby city centre for more than 30 years, with the last one finally going out of service on 9th September, 1967.

Above: Railway enthusiasts gathered at Derby Midland Station on 6th March, 1966, to greet a special visitor. The ex-London & North Eastern Railway Gresley Class A4 No 60019 "Bittern" paid a special visit to the city. The rail enthusiasts gathered to photograph this rare visitor, which had plied its trade on the East Coast rather than the Midland main line. The final few A4s - including 60019 - were later used on express passenger work between Glasgow and Aberdeen. All were eventually taken out of service during 1966. No 60019 was purchased privately for preservation. Designed by Sir Nigel Gresley, Bittern was built at the LNER works in Doncaster at the end of 1937. The locomotive was numbered 4464 and painted garter blue. The name comes from the bird of the same name. Many of the Gresley A4s were named after birds, including the famous record breaking Mallard. Bittern became one of a "flock" of 35 Gresley A4s, which in their prime served the famous LNER train services from London. Soon after the second world war the railways were nationalised and Bittern was renumbered 60019 under the British Railways scheme. It was sold privately in September 1966. It has seen had several owners since and spent time at the National Railway Museum. Since 2000 it has been at the Mid-Hants Railway (the Watercress Line) and has been undergoing a major restoration.

BIRDS EYE VIEW

Everything looks different from the air, but this aerial view of Victoria Street taken in the 1950s gives a clear impression of the sweep of the street and some of its grand buildings. Two of those notable buildings are seen in this view, with impressive and imposing Victoria Street Congregational Church clearly seen on the left and opposite it the former Post Office. The latter was built between 1865 and 1869 and opened as Derby's main post office on Thursday, December 1st, 1870. It remained as such until 1997, when the post office relocated into the former tramways offices in Victoria Street. Newcastle-based pub chain Ultimate Leisure Group plc bought the building in June 2003 and invested around £3 million converting it into a new bar. The church was demolished in 1962 and a new church built which later became the Central United Reformed Church.

Left: What extraordinary changes have been witnessed by those who have lived through the post war decades in Derby. Few changes have been more dramatic than those revealed by this photograph which shows the majestic sweep of the roads as the city's 1960s 'vision of tomorrow' became our today. In the latter half of the 20th the car would become the single thing which would come to dictate the shape of all of Britain's cities, not least Derby. Massive road improvement programmes would be initiated to cope with a massive increase in traffic. Yet today what seemed like overkill at the time now seems barely adequate.

Below: The tower of the Church of All Saints, second highest in England after the Boston Stump, still dominates the scene from Corporation Street, taken from The Council House, looking straight down Full Street. Now was the time of demolition. Our needs were changing, so the Assembly Rooms have been re-assembled (left). In 1967 the church of St Alkmunds was in the way of the proposed Inner Ring Road. The moving finger writes that where it stood is now a part of the new St Alkmunds Way. Derby power station, built in 1920, was closed in 1970. That's the police station on the right of the picture. The Derby Corporation vehicles parked in the foreground show the value of good planning.

This panoramic view is of Derby as it stood on the brink of the second world war, looking at the City Centre from the majesty of its cathedral tower. What draws the eye immediately is the light coloured building at centre picture which represents the handsomely copper topped dome of the Corn Exchange building which first shone golden in the sun on Albert Street in 1861. Diagonally down right is the huge single span saddle-roof of the Indoor Market Hall. Continuing the line down right you can admire the magnificence of the Guildhall with its domed

clock tower rising over a hundred feet and dominating the entire foreground of the picture. Next to it on your right are the bow-fronted windows of the Derby newspaper offices. Returning to the Exchange building at centre, to your left is the Council House under construction. Before it, diagonally down left, is the Phillipson store and still on the same line is the old Assembly Rooms building. In all this we can find evidence of the hopes and aspirations of the builders of Derby. It's a jigsaw of many pieces about who dared and won their moment in the history of a great city.

WORKING LIFE

Messrs Rolls and Royce were first introduced to each other at a meeting at the Midland Hotel in Manchester in May 1904. Henry Royce made cars and Charles Rolls sold them. Henry Royce's dictate was 'Whatever is rightly done, however humble, is noble'. He dictated that every single car part should receive meticulous care, both in design and construction. 'Strive for perfection in everything you do. Take the best that exists and make it better. When it does not exist, design it. Accept nothing nearly right or good enough.' The first product of the new partnership was the 40/50hp car, one of which was dubbed by Rolls-Royce Managing Director, Claude Johnson, the Silver Ghost. The Silver Ghost was the company's sole model from 1906 until 1922. It was a six-cylinder car with a seven-litre engine, hugely powerful for the time. Already by 1908, demand was so high for the new Rolls-Royce car that production had grown too large for the modest Manchester factory where it all began. A move was made to specially built premises on Nightingale Road in Derby, where car manufacture continued until 1939, and where the first aeroplane engines were made in 1915. The photograph at the bottom of the page shows the Nightingale Road production line in Derby in 1919. Nearly 8,000 of these cars would be made. When the Ghost was described by Daily Mail founder Alfred

Harmsworth as 'the best car in the world', Rolls Royce's reputation for uncompromising quality was sealed. Sadly Charles Rolls was not to live long enough to fully appreciate what he had achieved. On 12th July 1910 he was killed in a tragic flying accident. It was the influence of a trio of brothers from Derby who had first kindled Rolls' interest in flying. Leonard, Albert and Oswald Short lived in Fria

Gate Derby. In 1897 they took up ballooning and within thee years were building their own craft which Rolls took great interest in. In 1908 after witnessing a demonstration of the Wright brothers' new heavier than air flying machine Eustace Short offered to build six Wright Flyers at the Short's balloon works at Shellbeach in Kent. On 8th October 1908 Wilbur Wright personally took up Charles Rolls for his first flight. The close friendship between Rolls and the Wright brothers is witnessed by a famous photograph, above, showing Charles Rolls outside the Shellbeach works in his new Derby-made Silver Ghost, accompanied by Orville and Wilbur Wright. Rolls bought the first and sixth aircraft of the world's first aviation production line. He took to the air almost immediately making the first ever double crossing of the Channel in June 1910. On 11th June 1910, flying at an air display at Southbourne near Bournemouth, Rolls attempted, though just failed

to achieve, the world altitude record. The following day Rolls' plane crashed as he came into land: he died almost instantly; though aged only 32 he had, with Henry Royce, already done sufficient for their names to have become immortal.

Pictures below is Rolls Royce's Silver Ghost at a Rally of Rolls Royce cars at the Sinfin Works in the 1970s.

Below: In 1938 Vic Hallam Ltd purchased 11 acres at Langley Mill, at a cost of £1,400. The site included the New Inn, which was to be used as offices. A new factory was built, but before Hallam's could move in it was requisitioned by the Government for a munitions firm, Collaro, which had been bombed out of its premises in London. Collaro's manufactured shell cases and bullets amongst other things. Here girls with boiler suits were doing their bit for the country. In 1946, after the end of the war, Hallam's finally moved into the premises they had bought eight years earlier, and its other site at Marlpool closed. The company extended its range of products to include luxury items, such as radio cabinets. As success continued, the Langley Mill site was extended. The company, and the site at Langley Mill, was finally closed in 1995. It is now the location of the Access26 Business Park.

Left: In the days long before the National Health Service, hospitals had to find their own funding as this leaflet clearly shows. It was published for the Derbyshire Royal Infirmary and aimed to raise money to help with treatment for soldiers wound during the first world war. The leaflet was published during one of the bloodiest years of the war. It was the years that saw the notorious Battle of the Somme, which lasted from 1st July to 18th November. One of the most important campaigns in which the British Army has ever been engaged, the dogged fighting on the Somme has shaped modern memory of the first world war. The offensive campaign of 1916 - initially conceived by the French Commander-in-Chief to be a war-winning simultaneous strike on three fronts by all Allies with maximum force - came down to a few divisions of the British Army attacking on ground not of their choosing and where there was no possibility of strategic gain. After a terribly costly opening of the British attack, the Allied offensive pushed on yard by yard through a hot summer and eventually halted as the mud of winter closed in. In strategic terms little ground had been taken, but the German army had been seriously damaged and the British learned many lessons that would be applied in 1917 and 1918.

The gas industry was very different to what we know it today when these pictures were taken. It was in the second decade of a nationalisation and long before privatisation of gas supplies and services. The Derby area received its gas through the East Midlands Gas Board and it was even before North Sea gas came on the scene. Gas was popular for cooking, and most cookers and fires were bought from local gas showrooms. But with the constant battle to beat electricity, gas board chiefs had to think of ways to promote the business. They came up with this idea for a mobile gas showroom in the 1960s, so potential customers did not need to go the showrooms, the sales staff brought the showroom down their streets.

Above: There is a tradition of caring about Full Street which is clearly demonstrated in this picture dating back to end of the first world war in 1918. It shows children seated round a dinner table at the Women's Hostel on Full Street, with three nurses in attendance. The actual building is likely to have been demolished when the Assembly Rooms were built. But the caring tradition goes back far further. The street had centuries before housed the original Devonshire Almshouses which had been built by Bess of Hardwick. They were later rebuilt in the 1770s by the Countess of Shrewsbury. The caring tradition has a famous connection too. There is a statue of Florence Nightingale in London Road. Florence Nightingale was born in Italy on 12th May, 1820 and was named Florence after the city where she was born. On returning to England the Nightingales divided their time between two homes.

In the summer months they lived at Lea Hurst in Derbyshire, moving to Embley in Hampshire for the winter. Lea Hurst is now a retirement home and Embley is now a school. She provided books for Lea Primary school and provided the services of a doctor for the village poor. Once a year, star pupils of the school were invited to tea at Lea Hurst.

Below: The automatic car wash was still relatively new in the 1960s so when one opened at the British Car Auctions site at Measham, it was decided a special promotion was needed. The model girls were called it to pose for this picture taken around the early 1960s and also featured is one of the iconic cars of that time, the Minivan. BCA (British Car Auctions) is Europe's number one vehicle remarketing company, with more than 40 auction centres across the UK and Europe and a market-leading online presence. BCA turns over more than £3 billion annually.

Handling over one million vehicles per year. BCA sells vehicles from all sources (fleet, lease, contract hire, rental, manufacturer and dealer) primarily to professional trade buyers. The Measham site south of Derby has seen a number of special selling events over the years. It was the site chosen when the infamous DeLorean factory closed in Northern Ireland. While most of the completed vehicles went to the United States, a few DeLorean cars ended up staying in the UK when they were auctioned off at Measham car auctions by the receivers.

Left: These smart men of the Derbyshire County Constabulary posed for this picture some time in the early part of the 20th century, probably at the headquarters in St Mary's Gate, which are now offices for the magistrates' court. The Derbyshire Constabulary was formed in March 1857 with 156 men. There were eight divisions covering Ashbourne, Chesterfield, Derby, Glossop, Melbourne and Matlock. The force headquarters was originally at Belper but this proved unsuitable as it was also the divisional HQ and so the constabulary moved its base to Derby two years later - first to St James' Terrace and then relocating to St Mary's Gate in 1861. All ranks were expected to carry out their beat duties on foot, except for superintendents who were afforded the luxury of a pony and trap to get around. Officers and constables would communicate by telegram

or letter in those early days. Telephones were installed at divisional headquarters during the 1890s, something which was revolutionary at the time. The year 1931 saw the introduction of motorcycles and sidecars for the first motor patrols. Later police travelled around in Austin and MG sports cars. When the police headquarters in Derby became too small in 1958 the force moved to Matlock, followed by another move to Ripley in 1970. Today there are four divisions within the Derbyshire Constabulary: Alfreton, Buxton, Chesterfield and Derby. There were also separate borough forces, including ones for Derby, Chesterfield and Glossop. The latter two merged with Derbyshire Constabulary in 1947. Derby had its own police force until 1967 when it too amalgamated with the county constabulary.

Derbyshire Fire & Rescue
Nine-Nine-Nine 365 24/7

Derby Fire Brigade came into existence in 1837 as a result of a new Government policy imposing a requirement on local authorities to take responsibility for fire-fighting in their areas. This was due to an increasing number of fires throughout the country, and inadequate provision being made by insurance companies and locally run brigades. The local brigades were administered mainly by the church. The response to calls came from church bells ringing alarms and to shouts for help. Volunteers were paid 6d and a drink to 'man the pumps'. Before 1837 Derby had five separate fire engines operated by the churches of All Saint's, St Werburgh's, St John's, St Peter's and St Mary's.

The local council followed Government policy and ordered an inspection of the existing five fire engines. Only two of those horse-drawn and hand-operated pumps were found to be sufficiently serviceable to be of use in the new organisation. Both engines were housed and operated from premises in Tenant Street in Derby. An 'engine man' was engaged who lived close to the engine house. His wages were paid out of the salary of the Mayor.

An early problem for the brigade was the provision of water for fire-fighting: although the area of the Market Place had the nearby river Derwent, all other outlying areas had to rely on 'bucketing' from any available supply.

Around 1861, the engine house relocated to Full Street - a purpose built house in which the engineer lived on site. A

lack of investment in new equipment, however, resulted in a slow deterioration of the engines up until a disastrous fire at the Town Hall in 1866.

Arising from the Town Hall fire came a new commitment to invest: new fire engines were purchased, firemen employed and water mains laid. The period up to 1891 saw many changes in Derby including the growth of the railways and other industries. Many fires still occurred: the authorities were lobbied to stop properties being built too close together, using poor construction, and not including fire breaks, particularly where thatch roofs were involved. The introduction of steam-operated fire pumps provided spectacular viewing as the steaming, smoke-belching pumps careered through the town drawn behind galloping horses.

Derby gained a magnificent new fire station on Jury Street in the central area of the town in 1891. This purpose-built accommodation housed three fire engines with firemen's houses attached to the rear stretching towards Walker Lane and Willow Row. The houses on Jury Street all had bells to summon crews: one can imagine the effect on their families during busy times!

There were many outbuildings at Jury Lane to cater for horses, hay and animals: the fire brigade disposed of unwanted animals at this time. That unusual service continued well into the next century, the unfortunate animals being disposed of by electrocution.

During this period, the Police and Fire Brigade also shared some duties, and firemen were expected to transport prisoners to attend Nottingham Court.

Following the outbreak of the first world war in 1914, the brigade was badly depleted as a result of military service: luckily there were no major fires at that time. This period also saw the introduction of motorised appliances with pneumatic tyres. Some old crews still preferred the horses and it took many years to overcome their dislike of modern technology. Inevitably, however, all the horse drawn engines were withdrawn and replaced by two pumping appliances and one high-rise ladder.

In the early 1940s, during the second world war, cities like Coventry suffered major air attacks, and, as a result, fire appliances from all over the Midlands, including Derby went to help fight the conflagrations. These years also saw a massive influx of personnel into the Brigade including full

Facing page and above: Early photographs of the old Nottingham Road Fire Station and firefighters having a leisurely game of snooker accompannied by a tune from the piano.

of having three stations, all on main traffic routes, providing a rapid response to the suburbs or town centre.

In 1974, local government re-organisation required the Borough Brigade to join forces with the Derbyshire Fire Service that covered the rest of the county. The Derbyshire Fire Service name remained until recent years when the addition of 'Rescue' was adopted by most fire brigades.

That same year, the new headquarters opened at the Old Hall, Burton Road, Littleover in Derby where it remains to this day. The original Old Hall was built in 1607 by Richard Harpur, then demolished in 1890 and completely rebuilt to form the present house.

time, part time and members of the Auxiliary Fire Service using the 'green goddess' major pumps (these appliances and crews remained attached to Jury Street on a part time basis up until the mid sixties).

After the war, Derby began to grow and the resources of the brigade were increased to reflect this. The Fire Services Act of 1947 created the County Borough of Derby Fire Brigade, which replaced the National Fire Service that had performed so gallantly in the war years.

Due to increasing traffic congestion, Jury Street station was no longer best sited to cover all areas of the town. With expanding suburbs, another station was obviously required. A new fire station at Nottingham Road was opened in 1951 providing two more fire appliances. In 1963, yet another fire station opened at Ascot Drive which became the brigade headquarters.

In the 1930s the building was sold to Rolls Royce, which used it as a training establishment for foreign buyers of their aircraft engines. In 1972, 'a modern laboratory block, fully equipped canteen, attractive lodge and approximately 9.80 acres of land.' were bought by the County Council for the Fire Service.

Derby still has the three fire stations, although additional facilities at Kingsway now include a purpose built training complex for recruits and also breathing apparatus/real fire training. The headquarters site provides accommodation for

Fire brigade pumps, ladders and personnel are, however, not just used for putting out fires. The middle of the 1960s saw large scale flooding around the area of Chester Green, to which the brigade responded for days on end in the rescue of residents and animals.

Meanwhile, the old station at Jury Street was showing its age: a new station at Kingsway finally replaced it in 1968. This completed the overall strategy

a range of support departments and classroom-based training. All emergency calls are received at the Fire Control Centre at headquarters and appliances mobilised to incidents covering the whole county. Close liaison is maintained with the police and ambulance services to provide a inter-agency response to emergencies where appropriate.

public education to prevent accidents occurring.

The fire and rescue service works in partnership with a number of other agencies to deliver a range of services addressing community safety, anti-social behaviour and general well-being.

Derbyshire Fire and Rescue Service aspires to be one of the best performing services in the country and is well on the way to achieving that goal. The city of Derby has played a significant part in the progress of the fire and rescue service since the hand pumps of 1837: today the service is still committed to serving and caring for the population of the city every single day, hour and minute of the year.

The Nottingham Road station, built in 1951, is the first to be replaced as part of a new building programme, with a purpose-built community fire station opening in January 2008. Ascot Drive Fire Station, built in 1963, is due to be replaced in the near future.

Today's service is very different from that of yesteryear. As a result of the Fire and Rescue Services Act, 2004, and the Emergencies Order, 2007, the service now has a duty to respond to road traffic collisions and various major disasters as well as delivering fire safety education to local communities. Accordingly, vehicles, equipment, and training now reflect the need to deal with a wide variety of calls for assistance and greater emphasis is placed upon

Top left: An old view the Central fire station in Jury Street. Bottom left: Firefighters extinguishing a fire at a scrap metal works in Derby. Above: The Youth Engagement Scheme at Staveley. Below: An Emergency Services Event at Market Place, Derby, 2007.

The Parry Group - Sparks of Innovation

Today's Parry Group Ltd based in Town End Road, Draycott, Derby began its life in 1942 as a partnership between Jack Parry and Henry Martin, both previously employees of Ericsson's Telephones Ltd. They set up their business on a part-time basis in small, scattered buildings at Beeston, Nottingham, sub-contracting for coil windings used in telephone relays.

Coils for customers in the telephone industries and football turnstile counting equipment predominated in company's early ledgers.

In 1948 the inconvenient Beeston Works were abandoned and the move made to Victoria Mills in Townend Road, Draycott. Only three out of 28 rooms there were available, but as the rest were vacated the firm took them all over and bought the whole mill and began to diversify.

Within the space of two years Parry's was the largest independent producer of discharge lamp control gear in the UK, employing 370 people at Draycott and 100 at Stapleford, where Parry's Mechanical Engineering Department were marketing a range of fancy goods such as letter racks, nests of trays and fruit baskets under the 'Artstyles' name. The company's output had increased 17 times - with a workforce that had merely doubled.

Parry's began to exhibit at the Gothenburg Light Show and Hanover International Trade Fair. An integral unit for a mercury vapour lamp proved to be a particular success. The easily-fitted unit did away with the need for large numbers of conventional

Top: Jack Parry (far left) and Henry Martin (second right) co founders of the company. *Below:* A 1940s view of the W J Parry premises.

event at Olympia, aimed at the Catering and Hotel industry.

In the mid 1970s W J Parry Domestic Products Ltd had set up a plant in Pinxton to produce energy-saving vacuum cleaners. These were light in weight, and were given the descriptive name of Light n' Easy.

Through the 1980s business boomed. The fully automated Victoria Mills PARMAR plant at Draycott continued to develop its fluorescent units, and its sodium and mercury vapour control gear for works and street lighting. The new London Bridge, built around 1980, was lit using control gear from Parry's. More than a million units were produced every year.

lights in premises such as garages and workshops. Substantial export orders began to come in from Portugal, Sweden, Southern Ireland, Singapore, Australia and Jamaica. Within a few years the company was announcing export sales of £500,000.

In the late 1960s Parry's innovations in fluorescent lighting were made enabling fluorescent tubes up to a length of 4ft to be used in boats, caravans and public transport.

The company now took over a knitwear company in the mill. Unfortunately by January 1971 knitwear orders were thinning and the shortage of work led to redundancies. A month later the knitwear division closed down.

The mechanical side of the business, however, was doing well. The company's main works at Draycott had four floors totalling 100,000 sq ft. The tool room and press shops were housed there, as was the lighting products assembly. 1970 saw the concentration of the business at the Draycott factory, and the electro plating plant at Nottingham Road Stapleford was sold off.

Business in Australia was growing, and exports to the country had totalled around £90,000 in 1972. Plans were afoot to set up a new manufacturing subsidiary in Australia. The developments followed Parry's growth in South Africa, when Parry South Africa Pty Ltd was established to manufacture and assemble parts.

In 1972 the company purchased (Ridgeway) Catering Equipment Division, making catering equipment, selling through distributors to pubs, motorway service areas and thousands of small catering establishments. Sales continued to rise, and the equipment was exhibited at Hotelympia, a bi-annual

Recognising the future potential in electronics, the firm expanded into premises on the other side of the road. The modern single-storey 14,000 sq ft building was developed especially to manufacture electronic items. The final stage involved landscaping the development. Trees and shrubs were planted in an attractive layout to screen the new site.

The space vacated in the main works was put to good use, and the catering equipment division was expanded. Gas griddles and chargrills, food displays, heavy duty fryers, pizza showcases and coffee machines were just a few of the products. An experienced sales team provided advice on the planning of restaurants, pubs, cafes and clubs.

*Top: An aerial view of Victoria Works. **Below:** Salvage operation in the mill following a fire in the 1950s.*

The heavy duty design, sleek, attractive looks, and a design aimed towards the elimination of grease and dirt traps attracted attention, and in the mid 1990s Parry Catering Equipment Ltd was awarded the prestigious award BS5750, presented to the company by Home Secretary Kenneth Clarke.

Meanwhile room was left on the new site to more than double the works area and to erect an office block; this work was completed in the 1990s. A new division, PARMAR Distribution supplying Lighting Control Gear to the wholesale trade, began trading in 1992. A London Branch was opened in 1996.

In June 1997 the Lighting Control Division and the Mill were sold to an American Company, ADLT, and W.J. Parry relocated to the New Factory and the Artstyles Division moved to Castle Donington.

Parry's continued to expand through acquisitions. In 1998 it purchased a small electrical distribution company called Lyne Components Ltd. It was based in Corby, Northamptonshire and supplied lighting control gear and gear trays to the electrical wholesale industry and sign manufacturers. This acquisition was an excellent fit with the successful Parmar Distribution division.

In 1999 Parry's purchased a small steel fabricator based in Long Eaton. It manufactured a variety of bespoke steel fabrications for many different applications including fire escapes, security fencing and gates. The acquisition also secured the supply of griddle plates for the Parry Catering Equipment division.

Parry's made two more acquisitions in October 2000. The first of these was another steel fabrication company, Goodwin & Crossley, based on Harrington Street in Derby. The business

*Top: A staff party circa 1960s. **Below:** Parry Group Chairman Archie Stubbs (left) and Financial Director Gary Rose pictured during a series of open days to celebrated the company's 60th Anniversary.*

by the end of October 2003 making the factory some 45,000 square feet in total.

In October 2004 due to customers moving business to China and Eastern Europe, and the introduction of modern technology, the Board reluctantly had to close the metal pressings division, Artstyles, and the recent acquisition, Amberlight Engineering Ltd. The Steel Fabrications division moved into the Draycott factory where it became integrated with the Parry Catering Equipment division.

The following month the company invested £500,000 in a fully automated CNC punching cell. This was a crucial investment for the company's long-term survival. The machine was capable of running unmanned and could feed itself with material, punch the parts, pick the parts, place them on a pallet and take the scrap away.

manufactured stainless steel tables, canopies and shelving for the catering industry. The company was merged with the fabricator bought the previous year.

The second acquisition was Amberlight Engineering Ltd based in Matlock. This was a small precision engineering company with over 50 years experience that could manufacture precision tubular components to almost any size. In 2001 the business was moved to Via Gellia Mills in Bonsall near Matlock.

The Group was now made up of six companies. In 2001 the Group closed the London branch for its Parmar Distribution division since a pick up service in London was no longer required.

In March 2001 both steel fabrication companies relocated to Castle Donington Factory to join the metal pressings division, Artstyles.

The Lyne Components business was moved from Corby to Draycott and merged with the Parmar Distribution division in 2002.

During 2002 the Parry Catering division expanded with the introduction of various European products including dishwashers, refrigeration equipment, icemakers, combination steam ovens and meat-slicers - the Parry Plus range. The idea behind this was a 'one stop shop strategy'. A £1,000,000 turnover was achieved in the first year.

Space was becoming a problem at the Draycott headquarters so the factory was extended again. Another 4,000 square feet were added at the front of the building. The extension was completed

Parry Catering now has over 800 distributors throughout the UK and Parry Electrical has over 2,000 customers.

The Group now employs around 90 people: several of whom have over 35 years of service. Parry's is very proud of that fact, and is keen to maintain the family culture that has been built up over 60 years.

Parry's has long had a determination to be first in the field with production techniques, new developments and innovations, while at the same time maintaining quality and increasing capacity. For the future Parry's has plans to expand the product range of both of its companies and is looking forward to growing, developing and facing the challenges ahead.

Top: *Interior (inset) and exterior views of the company premises.* **Centre:** *A Parry Catering's salad cart.* **Below:** *Parry's showroom.*

The University Of Derby - Learning For Life

In Derby, 150 years ago, several educational traditions began to trace a route toward what was destined to become the present day University of Derby – one of the UK's most innovative seats of modern higher learning. In the 1850s the first higher education institution was founded in Derby, for the training of women teachers; that was soon joined by a school to provide Derby's workers with specialist vocational design skills demanded by some of the most advanced businesses of that industrious age. Within 20 years art and design formed one focus and science another, while the education of teachers continued to thrive. Just over a century later, provision in art, science, health, technology and education were brought together in one higher education institution in Derby. University status was granted by the Privy Council in 1992.

An Engine Of Creativity

The Industrial Revolution brought mass migration from the countryside, and towns grew fast. Between 1800 and 1835 Derby's population swelled by 20,000 and new social challenges associated with overcrowding and rapid technological change began to emerge. In 1825, the Mechanics' Institution was established, with the support of the celebrated Strutt family of textile entrepreneurs, to deliver scientific lectures to workers in Derby. When the railway came to Derby in 1835 it was one of the most significant events in the city's history. This introduced 'high technology', heavy industry and increased demand for specialist skills. The Mechanics' Institution hosted the first classes to teach these skills and supported the creation of new schools.

The Foundation Of An Educational Ethos

As Derby grew, enlightened educational reformers sought to establish schools, not only for the privileged few but also for the children of workers, which – of course – required trained teachers. The Bishop of Lichfield, John Lonsdale, recognised this need and set about providing for it. The Diocesan Institution for the Training of School Mistresses was created in 1851: it arose from a desire to provide opportunities for women to realise their potential even when denied the benefits of a university education. It was the first founding institution of the University of Derby.

This progressive attitude towards opening access to higher education is another hallmark of the modern University of Derby's mission. The Institution was built on Uttoxeter New

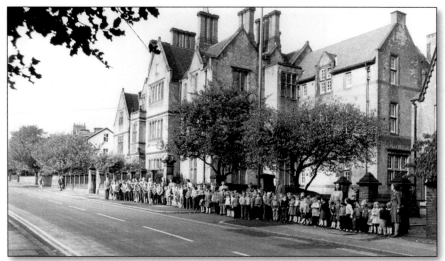

art teachers at the Diocesan Institution, the First Derby School of Art declined and closed in 1870.

Arts And Sciences In Parallel

Derby Central School of Art and Derby Central School of Science came into being separately in 1870. The School of Art at first occupied unsuitable premises, but a site for its new home was found at Green Hill (latterly known as Green Lane) and a fine High Victorian-Gothic building was opened in June 1877 by the 7th Duke of Devonshire, a generous supporter of education in Derbyshire and Chancellor of the Universities of Cambridge and London. This building continued to be the focus of arts teaching for 120 years.

A meeting at Derby Guildhall in November 1883 recorded workers commenting on what university 'extension' education should be brought to Derby. They were keen to insist on 'technical' education rather than 'scientific' education, desiring classes relevant to their circumstances. An influential report at the time endorsed the need for high standards of technical education, so the Central School of Art became the Derby School of Art and Technical Institution to reflect this. The separate School of Science, housed in the Old Derby Grammar School at St. Peter's Churchyard, also focused more on technical instruction.

In 1888, the School of Art merged formally with the School of Science to become the Derby Central School of Science and Art and Technical Institution. Well-regarded courses continued to thrive in Derby and some were validated externally as degrees, mainly by London University. In the 1890s one of the earliest subject areas to be offered to degree level was Geology. Other

Road and developed so quickly that its first extension was required only seven years after the original building was completed, in 1858. In the next 60 years a chapel, a gymnasium, a practicing school and a practicing infants' school were added, anticipating the modern University of Derby's provision of realistic working environments offering a combination of higher education and advanced vocational training.

In 1927 Derby became a separate diocese and the Institution was renamed the Derby Diocesan Training College. Its first woman principal, Miss H K Hawkins, urged her students to "develop that personality and spirituality, which make education a reality." Throughout the mid 20th century, the College continued to develop and expand. In 1965 under Principal Amy Sefton it became the Bishop Lonsdale College of Education. Shortly afterwards it moved to a new purpose-built campus at Mickleover and admitted male students for the first time.

A Call For Art And Design Skills

Over the past two centuries in Derby, educators have kept pace with the needs of the local population and of employers. Makers of textiles, porcelain and timepieces have been joined by bankers, rail and then aerospace engineers, specialist providers of healthcare, IT and creative entertainment innovators, and a burgeoning service sector. Derby adapted to changing educational needs and most of its further and higher education institutions have consolidated to become this University.

A demand from local employers for design skills inspired Derby Mechanics' Institution to deliver drawing classes for workers. One of the instructors, in 1847, was London artist Augustus Oakley Deacon. Shortly afterwards, a permanent tradition of art teaching was founded in Derby with the First (also known as the 'Old') Derby School of Art. Deacon became its first Headmaster. The School ran from 1853 to 1870. It was a private enterprise, set up, among other things, to provide drawing instruction for trainee teachers at the Diocesan Institution for the Training of School Mistresses as well as answering the need to teach drawing skills to support local industries. With the appointment of two

Left: An early view inside Derby Central School of Art. *Above:* The original home of the Diocesan Institution for the Training of School Mistresses. *Below:* Students outside Fitzherbert Hall, Mickleover, in the 1970s.

areas, such as Photography, would achieve national and international recognition in the 20th century, and were early drivers in Derby's bids to award its own higher education qualifications.

In the 1890s, the municipality of Derby took over responsibility for art, science and technical education, and schools teaching those disciplines came together for the first time. In the 1920s art and technology were separated out again, and in 1925 new engineering laboratories were opened at Normanton Road. The late 1920s saw a University for the East Midlands proposed, in which Derby would have had a University College, but by 1930 this dream had faded. Additional degree subjects began to be taught at Derby but awarded by external bodies, such as Chemistry, validated by the Royal Institute of Chemistry. It would be another 60 years before Derby became a university, through considerable hard work and determined leadership.

Towards Consolidation

During the 20th century names changed and other institutions were absorbed. Work on a large new site on Kedleston Road at Allestree to accommodate a College of Technology alongside a College of Art began in 1957 and was completed in 1965. Since engineering laboratories were opened at Normanton Road in 1925 by Sir Charles Parsons, inventor of the steam turbine, apprentices from Rolls-Royce, British Rail Engineering, and other industrial concerns had studied to diploma and degree level part time at 'The Tech'. This close relationship with major employers remains a key part of what Derby does well. A respected Foundation degree in Manufacturing and Mechanical Engineering is still delivered in conjunction with Rolls-Royce and Derby College, and a wide range of other employers work with the University through its *Times Higher Education Supplement* Award-winning Learning Through Work team.

Top left: Kedleston Road, 1970s. *Top right:* Derby University's Learning Centre. *Right:* Professor John Coyne with Sir Richard Branson at the Official Opening of the new Markeaton Street site in Derby.

Derby College of Art and Technology was formed by an amalgamation of the two colleges at Kedleston Road in 1972, and academic faculties were first created in a full restructure. In 1977, Derby Lonsdale College of Higher Education was created as a unique independent trust incorporated the former municipal Derby College of Art and Technology and the Church of England Bishop Lonsdale College, with three Bishops and three County Councillors as Trustees. The institution was further extended in 1983 by incorporating Matlock College of Higher Education into the renamed Derbyshire College of Higher Education. By the end of the 1980s Derbyshire College of Higher Education had a wide range of HND and professional courses in Engineering and Business Studies, but only seven first degree programmes; four validated by the Council for National Academic Awards (CNAA) and three validated by Nottingham University. The Director of the college, Jonathan May, proclaimed it "a polytechnic in all but name", but serious progress towards that goal wasn't made until 1989. The 1980s were a tough time, with major budget cuts for the College. Nonetheless, areas such as Textile Design garnered

awards and forged ahead, and new courses in computing were created.

Higher Education And Vocational Excellence

Under Director Roger Waterhouse, who arrived in 1989, assisted by Deputy Director Jonathan Powers, a flexible Credit Accumulation Modular Scheme (CAMS) became a major vehicle for growth of honours and masters degree programmes. In January 1991 a great fire destroyed engineering and textiles facilities at Kedleston Road, but progress continued. The College qualified for polytechnic status in 1992, however the Government suddenly decided to dissolve the line between polytechnics and universities.

Polytechnics were upgraded to universities, but Colleges wishing to gain university status now had to attain powers to award research degrees. Derby marshalled its resources to satisfy the CNAA that it should have research degree powers and it therefore became the only College of Higher Education to become a university at the same time as the former polytechnics. Following a successful external examination of the research training environment, Derbyshire College of Higher Education was redesignated a University in 1993.

The period of rapid expansion and creative development of the curriculum continued. Health became a major new addition to the University in the mid-1990s when the South West Trent School of Radiography, the Derby College of Occupational Therapy, the Medicines Research Unit, and allied programmes from the Derby College of Nursing joined the University. Radiography was based at the Derbyshire Royal Infirmary until early 2007 when it moved to a major new Clinical Skills Suite at Kedleston Road, a training facility emulating real hospital facilities. Occupational therapy was taught at the Cedars site on Whittaker Road until 2007, when it moved to the newly refurbished Britannia Mill.

Derby, Derbyshire... The World!

In 1998, High Peak College, at Harpur Hill on the outskirts of the spa town of Buxton joined the University. This was the first true merger across the higher education and further education sectors, creating a real centre of lifelong learning in the north of Derbyshire. Already a respected catering college running a wide range of further education courses, Buxton has since developed specialist higher education subjects that revolutionise whole industries like hair, beauty and spa. In 2000 Professor Roger Waterhouse took the opportunity to acquire the stunning Devonshire Royal Hospital. A five year restoration of the Grade II* domed building was steered through by Professor John Coyne when he joined as Vice-Chancellor in 2004. Their Royal Highnesses Prince Charles and Camilla, Duchess of Cornwall, opened the Devonshire Campus officially in 2006. Towards the end of that year the University's own training spa was created to support the world's first degree in International Spa Management.

In Derby, the School of Law – utilising the University's own Court Room – had, by 2007, become the most highly rated Law School in the country for student satisfaction. Professor Coyne continued to lead innovations and estates developments culminating, in 2007, with Derby's nomination as 'University of the Year'. A brand new £21m site at Markeaton Street consolidated Derby's estates in Derby, including Kedleston Road and Britannia Mill, in a University Quarter for the city.

As a consequence of its remarkable strengths and reputation the University now attracts students from over 100 countries. It has collaborative arrangements nationally and internationally as well, and has also been rated one of the 'greenest' universities in the UK.

Above and below: *The restored Grade II* domed building of the Devonshire Campus officially opened in 2006 by Their Royal Highnesses Prince Charles and Camilla, Duchess of Cornwall.*

The Midlands Co-operative Society Divi'ing Up History

Can you remember your Divi number? Readers who are old enough to understand the question will almost certainly be able to recall those vital digits. For more than a century Divvy numbers were an important part of shopping at the Co-op. Anyone – and that once meant almost everyone – could become a member of the Co-op. Profit sharing would be proportional to the amount members spent in the store. The more a member bought the more he or she would benefit. The pay-out was known as the dividend – more commonly known as the 'divvy'. But it was important to quote your Divvy number each time a purchase was made in order that it could be recorded against the member's account.

The divi, paid out four times a year, was a major event for Co-op members.

The Co-operative movement in England achieved its first success in the Lancashire town of Rochdale in 1844. It was there that a small group of 'co-operators' set up a shop to sell food at reasonable prices to members of the

Above: The first store in George Yard. **Right and below:** Early twentieth century stores.

'co-operative'. Soon the idea spread nationwide. In 1850 a group of carpenters and joiners holding a craft meeting in the Bull's Head pub in Queen's Street, Derby, decided to follow the example of the 'Rochdale Pioneers' and set up a small store in a converted hay loft above a stable in George Yard off Sadler Gate.

Initially the Derby Co-op only allowed carpenters and joiners to become members, but in 1859 membership was opened to all.

The first management committee was made up of the 12 original carpenters and joiners who founded it – they would be referred to by colleagues as the 'apostles'.

From its earliest days the Derby Co-op took a wide interest in its staff and members. Societies and clubs were formed which encouraged teamwork and good staff relations. One of the first such groups came in 1872 when 30 shillings (£1.50) was spent on establishing a Co-op Cricket Club. There would also be a Clothes Club, a Choral Society, a Women's Guild, a Men's Guild, Tennis Club, a Theatre Guild, and not least the Derby Co-op Football Team which played in the Wednesday League in the days when every shop in Derby closed on Wednesday afternoons.

In 1894 the Derby Co-op opened its first dairy, at Spondon, and in 1904 went on to start doorstep milk deliveries. Milk was ladled out from churns carried on handcarts. By the time the new dairy opened in Wood Street in 1935 the Society was supplying milk to almost three out of four Derby homes. Bread too was one of the Co-op's important products. In 1877 a Co-op bakery opened in Monk Street and bread deliveries too soon became a major activity. By the 1920s the Co-op could boast that it baked more bread than all the other bakers in Derby put together. The new Peak bakery opened at Osmaston Park Road in 1954 to supply a far wider market than just Derby.

The Co-op's interests went beyond life: its funeral services ensured that members could boost their divi even after death.

In the early 1900s the Co-op put a great deal of effort into creating good relations with the region's farmers: in turn the farmers gained a reliable and regular customer. The Co-op also had two farms of its own: Nottingham Road acquired in 1908, and Morley opened in 1920.

In another field entirely The Co-op Movement had always had a philanthropic purpose Initially this had meant strict party neutrality, but from the early 1900s there was increasing concern within the Derby Co-op that the town council was hostile to it.

Top left and above: Leisure time at Central Hall and the sports ground. Below left and below: Early views inside the dairy (left) and the bakery (below).

Inevitably the Co-op needed a large transport department. At first horses and carts were the order of the day, but in the years after the first world war a move was begun to switch to motor vehicles. By 1925 the Co-op had more than 60 motor vehicles in its fleet. Even so, much of the transport remained horse-drawn until after the second world war.

Many buildings in and around Derby remain a testament to the activities of the Co-op. The Derby Co-op had its own building department in the 1870s: its original job was to build houses for members, as well as being a building society for those wanting to borrow money to buy their own homes.

Many members were joining the still fledgling Labour Party. In 1918 the Derby Co-op decided to contest local elections and in doing so became affiliated to the Labour Party. In 1919 A.J. Tapping became Derby's first Co-op/Labour councillor. Not everyone, however, was happy: in the 1930s Lord Beaverbrook campaigned against the Co-operative Movement which he called the 'Co-octopus' and was successful in persuading the Government to tax the Co-op's previously exempt financial reserves.

Meanwhile, between the two world wars, the Co-op extended its public role even further: its Education Department ran night school classes.

Perhaps the most popular Co-op event of the year however was Penny Treat Day – an annual trip to the countryside. The 'Penny' referred to was the Penny Bank scheme, set up in 1875 to encourage thrift by inviting children to save a small amount of money each week. Penny Treat Day would later become the celebration of International Co-operators' Day and later a Co-op Fun Day.

Despite the Co-op's apparent robustness not everything, however, was plain sailing. On two occasions there were motions to disband the Society. In 1893 a rival tried to damage the Co-op by distributing leaflets claiming that the Co-op's prices were much higher than his own. The Co-op sued and won.

After 1894 the building department became a direct labour organisation which built new Co-op premises or converted existing buildings for Co-op use.

The Central Hall, completed at the outbreak of world war one was built by that direct labour organisation. Other examples were the Society's abattoir and dairy completed in the 1930s.

Underlying everything, however, remained a commitment to the original egalitarian principles. All members had equal voting rights. Until the 1960s members were even able to vote for people to fill the top jobs in the Society, including its General Manager.

Though Derby's Co-op existed in its own right it was also a member of the Co-operative Movement's bodies. Derby would become home to several elements of that national supply chain. The Peak Bakery and the CWS (Co-operative Wholesale Society) Paintworks made products for the wider market. The paintworks had been set up in a former foundry in Stockbrook Street in the

Top left: A delivery vehicle unloading at the Co-op farm. Above: Home delivery vans load up orders before setting off on their rounds. Left: A view inside the Drapery Department in the 1950s.

1920s. Elsewhere the CWS Seed Trial Ground off Osmaston Park Road, which operated until the 1970s, produced seed potatoes and other seeds for sale nationally.

After a number of mergers, Derby Co-op is now part of Midlands Co-operative Society. Today with 37 trading outlets in Derby, Midlands Co-op has an important role within the community as so many people rely on the services it provides. The portfolio includes 15 retail outlets, three post offices, ten travel shops, six funeral homes, one florist and two masonry services!

The Department Store on Exchange Street, can fairly be described as the Co-op's flagship within the City. In March 2006 it completed a nine-month long programme of work that cost over £1.2m and transformed the store into a modern shopping environment, benefiting members, customers and staff alike. In addition to improving the store's layout and its product range, the works also included the upgrading of facilities, installation of air conditioning, updating of the fixtures and fittings with new technology introduced at till points. The exterior of the store was also given a new look to provide a more contemporary appeal.

That same year the Co-op opened a brand new £1 million convenience store on the corner of Mowbray Street and Osmaston Road. The 3,000 sq ft store occupies a former petrol station site and has brought much needed shopping facilities to the local community – as well as creating a number of employment opportunities.

In May 2007 the Midlands Co-op celebrated the opening of a larger store in Burton Road, Littleover. Having acquired the premises from another retailer earlier in the year, the Co-op gave the store a £300,000 makeover, closed its existing convenience store on 23rd May, and re-opened in the new store the next day.

The Midlands Co-op's success in Derby is a key component of its success as a Society – and its staff are proud of its role as a community retailer in a city that is facing the future with confidence: the Co-op is undoubtedly a force to be reckoned with.

Top left: *The Co-op central premises on Exchange Street.* **Above left:** *Peak Bakery pictured in the 1970s.* **Top right:** *A fun day out for the family on Co-op Fun Day.* **Below:** *Co-op Department Store, Derby (top left), Osmaston Road (top right), and the launch of the Littleover store (bottom left and bottom right).*

G Wathall - A Final Service

It was in 1858 that the cabinet-making and furniture-broking business established by Leonard Wathall in Siddalls Lane diversified into funerals. Leonard's son, George, established G Wathall & Son, the firm which continues to this day.

Since those early days five generations of the Wathall family have been involved in the firm, which today remains a family affair with Leonard's great-great granddaughter, Helen Wathall, now at the helm.

G Wathall & Son is the longest established independent funeral directors in Derby. The business has inevitably witnessed many changes during the last century and a half.

The first premises were in Green Street. Later there were offices in London Road, Normanton Road and Gerard Street. At the start of the 20th century premises were acquired in Macklin Street and this is where the business is still based today.

The Wathall family has absorbed and adapted to changes, over the years building a reputation for care for the deceased, concern for the bereaved, attention to detail, reliability and fair costs.

George Wathall, who died in 1898 at the impressive age of 77, was followed into the business by his son, William Henry, who died at the age of 61 in 1918. His sons, William and Henry (Harry) took over at a very young age and it was during their time at the helm that the firm witnessed the significant change from using horses to motor vehicles. Wathall's was one of the

first funeral directors in the area to use a motorised hearse. Prior to the introduction of motorised vehicles, the firm had about eight horses stabled at its Macklin Street premises.

During the first world war, the black Flemish horses were called up to serve with the Army. Harry, who fought in France with the Army, was captured by the Germans and held as a prisoner of war.

During the second world war the firm became part of a joint effort with other businesses in Derby to cover the possibility of civilian deaths due to any air raids on the town. Premises on Abbey Street were turned into a temporary mortuary. G. Wathall & Son Ltd held coffins in stock for the duration of the war in the event of Derby being targeted in large-scale air raids. Records of military funerals carried out during the war are still held by the firm.

The firm no longer owns any horses but hires them when they are requested. The stables now garage a fleet of nine Daimler and Mercedes hearses and limousines.

In 1952 Harry's son, William (Bill) joined the firm at the age of 20 having completed his National Service. William and Harry began to take a back seat until they both retired in the 1970s. Harry died in 1977, his brother two years later.

Bill Wathall, a qualified member of the British Institute of Embalmers, worked tirelessly for more than 40 years, latterly as chairman of the company until his death in 1995 at the age of 62. During his time, Bill gave many talks to local groups about his work and those talks are still fondly remembered.

Down the decades much has changed. All coffins were made on the premises until the 1980s. They are now bought in, although they are still lined on the premises.

The Management team currently comprises of Jean Wathall as Company Chairman, Helen Wathall, who has been with the company since 1985, as Company Secretary and Managing Director, Paul Edwards as Finance Director since 2001, and General Manager Mark Hodgson.

In 1995, G. Wathall and Son Ltd won the Golden Charter Funeral Planner of the Year Award for outstanding service, beating 1,900 other independent firms.

In 2002 Helen became the first woman to be elected President of the National Society of Allied and Independent Funeral Directors.

The firm opened a branch office at 5 Union Street, Ashbourne, Derbyshire in January 2007, a locality where the family has lived for more than 80 years.

Yet though much had changed the important things remain unaltered. G Wathall & Son's dedicated members of staff still provide their traditional, dignified, quality service, which the people of Derby and the surrounding areas have come to expect– 24 hours a day, 365 days a year.

Top left: Albert Street, Derby in 1927 – leading the cortege are Will and Harry Wathall. Left: A Shillibeer – both hearse and carriage - pictured at the rear of the Macklin Street premises. Above: Early photograph of the firm's Fleet of cars. Below: Will and Harry leading a cortege from Weston Street, Derby.

Thorntons - The Nicest Sweetshop in Town

To have 'the nicest sweet shop in town', was commercial traveller Joseph William Thornton's aim in 1911 when he decided to open his own shop, 'The Chocolate Kabin', at 159 Norfolk Street, Sheffield. Unfortunately, Joseph William died in 1919, at the relatively young age of 49, leaving his two sons Norman and Stanley to carry on the business.

Norman Thornton was born in Sheffield in 1896. He left Sheffield Grammar School when his father opened the sweet shop. Norman, then aged fourteen, was left to run the shop, while his father continued to work as a travelling salesman for the Don Confectionery Company.

Joseph Stanley Thornton, was born in 1903 and was also educated at Sheffield Grammar School. He won a scholarship to Sheffield University, but instead decided to work in the family business during the day, and study food technology, in particular confectionery-making, in the evenings.

Famed for its Special Toffee, the recipe Thorntons use today remains faithful to the one originally created in 1925 by Stanley. A perfectionist, it took him over 50 attempts to create a recipe that he thought was the correct taste and texture.

The first shop had brought in £20 a week, enabling the founder to open a second shop in 1913, on The Moor in Sheffield. The family moved to live over the shop, hand-rolling sweets, boiling mint rock over a gas fire in the basement, and hand-dipping violet creams. However, in the early days most of the confectionery sold was bought in.

Norman took over the business on his father's death in 1919, and opened two more Chocolate Kabins.

Norman, concentrating on the retailing side of the business, opened the first Thorntons shop outside Sheffield, in 1928, in Rotherham. By 1939 Thorntons had increased the number of shops to thirty-five, including the first Derby shop at 12 Market Place.

*Above: The original Chocolate Kabin. **Below left:** The Queen looks at a production line of rum truffles – all later destroyed for hygiene reasons. **Below:** Her Majesty was impressed by this 1.2 metre high chocolate bunny made at the Swanwick factory.*

In 1927 the brothers had moved production to a small factory in the Hillsborough area of Sheffield. It was at this time that Norman Thornton had the idea of icing customers' names on to Easter eggs whilst they waited, an idea which proved very successful. They moved to a bigger plant in 1931, and again in 1935, to a purpose-built factory in the Millhouses area of Sheffield, which was to be their headquarters until the 1980s.

With the end of sweet rationing in 1952, the firm began to expand again. In 1954 the Swiss Confisseur Walter Willen joined the company to develop Thorntons most popular range of chocolates, Continental. Maintaining the family business tradition, Norman and Stanley Thornton's sons joined the business during the 1950s.

Refused permission to extend the factory after the war, because of the shortage of building materials, Thorntons bought and moved to Castle Factory, near Belper, in Derbyshire.

In March 1985, Her Majesty the Queen opened Thornton Park, the purpose-built site near Alfreton and there was a sweet treat in store for her grandchildren. Swiss Confisseur Walter Willen, had specially iced the names Peter, Zara, William and Harry on to four special Thorntons Easter eggs. During the visit, the Queen watched rum truffles rolling off the production line - but in keeping with the stringent food hygiene rules these were later destroyed because the Royal party had not been asked to wear overalls. Her Majesty also saw a 1.2 metre high chocolate bunny that had taken Mr Willen and his team two weeks to make, using 24 coats of chocoate.

Barry Colenso, joined the business in the 1980s as Thorntons' Master Chocolatier, after working in a number of highly prestigious restaurants. This included the role as Chef Patissier at the Savoy Hotel, London. It was during his time at the Savoy that inspired the creation of Dessert Gallery, a sublime collection of dessert chocolates such as lemon meringue, tiramisu and creme brulee.

By 2007 Thorntons had over 580 shops in the UK and the Republic of Ireland, including 32 cafes, the first of which opened in 1996. Derby's first Café Thorntons opened in October 2007, featuring in the city centre's new Westfield shopping centre.

At Easter 2007, in the piazza at London's Covent Garden, Thorntons set up the world's first edible billboard. Using almost 400 kg of chocolate the structure featured 72 handmade Easter eggs and ten giant hand-crafted chocolate bunnies.

Thorntons is a big name in chocolate. Each shop continues to have the same aim as the founder, Joseph William - to be the nicest sweet shop in town!

Top left: Thorntons Confisseur Walter Willen with the four eggs he decorated for the Queen's grandchildren. Above: Barry Colenso pictured with the chocolate billboard. Below: Thorntons new Derby Westfield Café which opened in October 2007.

Image courtesy of Will Fenning of Fenning Brown Photography

Smith of Derby - Time Travellers

'What time is it?' A simple enough question, and one frequently answered by glancing upwards to check on the nearest church tower or town hall.

The first mechanical clocks appeared in England in the 13th century: their purpose was to automatically ring bells to mark the time monks and nuns should make their prayers. To the technically minded even today the word 'clock' specifically denotes a device which announces the time by striking a bell.

In the following centuries clocks became ever more sophisticated, and spread from religious buildings to secular ones. The sight of large clock faces prominently displayed on public buildings and other structures is so commonplace today that we seldom stop to give much thought to them. Yet not only are they an important part of daily life they also support and are supported by an army of skilled clockmakers and technicians ensuring that we continue to be able to enjoy and benefit from their presence.

Foremost amongst those who provide church and public clock restoration and service is the largest firm of tower clockmakers in Britain, Smith of Derby Group with its headquarters in Alfreton Road.

The Smith of Derby clock-making tradition has its roots in an even older business, which started with John Whitehurst the first in 1735, at 22 Irongate in Derby. It was his third successor who took on John Smith as an apprentice. John Smith left the Whitehurst firm to become a millwright but continued with clock repair work. His wife Maria dealt with customers and cleaned domestic clocks and watches during the day while John repaired and reassembled them in the evening. In the 1860s they rented, and later bought, 27 Queen Street from the Whitehurst family.

In the mid 19th century John Smith realised the business potential of large public clocks. He was fortunately placed near

*Top left: John Smith. **Below left:** The John Smith premises of 27 Queen Street, circa 1900. **Below:** Evidence of the ingenuity required by the itinerant clockmaker – here he seems to have borrowed part of an appliance from the fire Station to service the clock at Sheerness in Kent. The date is July 1933.*

the headquarters of the Midland Railway which became a major customer. John Smith built tower clocks for churches, town halls, stations and private houses throughout the United Kingdom and abroad. His clocks were, and still are, highly regarded for quality of manufacture, long service life and reliability. A major milestone was building the great clock of St Paul's Cathedral, London in 1893. This clock is still serviced by Smith of Derby and is now one of many thousands of clocks serviced in the British Isles.

From hand wound church clocks built by blacksmiths in the 1600s, to sophisticated devices made by celebrated 19th century clockmakers or the most modern electrically powered public clocks of the 21st century, the Smith of Derby Group can repair and service it. The Group's in-depth knowledge of historical clocks means that its staff can renovate virtually any mechanism.

The Smith Group's long standing traditions are still maintained through family ownership in the person of company Director Nicholas Smith, the fourth generation of the Smith family in the business - making the Smith of Derby Group the oldest firm of family owned clockmakers in the country. In 1998 the company moved to larger premises on Alfreton Road, Derby, where it continues to manufacture virtually all the parts which make up its diverse product range – an increasing rarity today.

In the 20th century John Smith & Sons expanded through the acquisition of other clockmakers. William Potts & Sons of Leeds, with a history of its own going back to 1833, was taken over in 1933. J B Joyce of Whitchurch, the oldest firm of tower clockmakers in the world and which had been trading since 1690, was acquired by the Smith Group on 1965, though continued to trade in its own right. The firm of G & F Cope was bought in 1984, whilst in the following year Smith's acquired B & H (Derby) Ltd, whose specialist metalwork skills continue to be in demand today in the building of major public art features such as the new globe for the London Coliseum.

Over the last 25 years the Smith of Derby Group has cleaned, repaired and overhauled in excess of 3,000 mechanical clocks. It has restored over 1,000 clock dials. Each year staff attend over 4,500 public and church clocks, in carrying out that service work the group's team of clockmakers drive more than 250,000 miles each year.

*Top left: Refitting the hands at St Paul's Cathedral after re-gilding in 1937. These hands were not removed for re-gilding again until 2003. **Above:** The Light Machine Shop at Queen Street in 1944. Left to right: Alf Jordan; Eric Ladds; Harry Farnsworth; Jim Hodgkinson; Arthur Humphries; Frank Hitchcock; Harold Lane. **Left:** F. W. "Pete" Dawkins gilding at Hugglescote Church, August 1954. The technique remains the same today using traditional top quality gold leaf. Health and safety requirements are however very different! **Below:** Installing the new globe for the London Coliseum in 2003. Today Smith of Derby's craftsmanship is applied to major landmark features.*

Moody & Woolley - Help with the Law

To most people the law is a mystery. Yet sooner or later everyone will become involved in matters which have some legal significance. And then we need a trusty guide to see us safe through the legal labyrinth.

A will may seem simple enough, but it needs someone who knows what they doing to help draw it up. The problems of inheritance tax and trusts are everyday problems to the solicitor, but without that expert help families could find themselves in a real pickle. House conveyancing is such a traumatic and potentially tricky area that it is one definitely best left to the professional. Who would want to risk the frightening prospect of facing a court room without legal support? If corporate giants turn their business contracts over to lawyers then the ordinary citizen are well advised to do the same. You would not dream of pulling your own teeth or teaching yourself to a science

degree, so why the reticence in drawing on other people's skills in the legal world? Certain firms of solicitors have specialist skills which their legal partners can draw on these to offer the very best service possible.

This is very much the case at Moody and Woolley. Not only does the firm have the expertise, it has the experience: over a century and a half of it. Queen Victoria was in her mid-20s when Frederick Baker set up as a solicitor in Bank Chambers, Cornmarket in 1846. When John Moody joined Baker at 20 Cornmarket in 1861 the firm became Baker and Moody. The older man died of rheumatic fever in 1864 and John Moody carried on singlehandedly. The business expanded and Moody gained a new partner in William Woolley in 1884. The names of Moody and Woolley were joined in the firm's title which has continued to be used to this day. John Moody died in 1889 and William Woolley continued on his own. At the turn of the century other partners were taken into the business and the firm grew in size and influence. Larger premises were needed to handle the level of business and a move was made to 40 St Mary's Gate in 1912, the week the Titanic sank! The grand Georgian residence, built in 1800, is where the firm remains to this day.

William Woolley's sons joined the firm, however only Leslie Woolley stayed long enough to have any significant

*Top: John Moody, who joined the firm in 1861. **Left:** St Mary's Gate c.1912, the year the firm took over the building on the right. **Below:** Members of staff in the late 1960s.*

influence. He became a partner in 1929 when most of the work in the office was still being recorded in longhand.

At that time typewriters, the high-tech machines of the time, were only starting to make a limited appearance; and until 1930 the firm had just one telephone in a specially soundproofed booth.

Leslie Woolley served his country as a captain in the Royal Artillery and after the war returned to the firm until his death in 1968.

In 1996 Moody and Woolley celebrated 150 years of legal service in Derby. It was an celebration attended by more than 100 members of firm, the oldest of whom could still remember the days when a man was employed specifically to keep the coal piled on the open fires situated in every room.

In the new millennium the firm expanded significantly in all departments, especially in commercial property, probate, tax, elderly client care as well as family law and child care. In addition a new personal injury department would be created

In 2003 the firm bought the adjoining premises – the old Probate Court in St Mary's Gate – almost doubling the office space. After restoration Derbyshire's Lord Lieutenant officially opened the building in December 2004.

When the firm celebrated its 160th anniversary in 2006 it held a grand fancy dress party at which guests wore costumes covering the whole period of the firm's existence.

Today, Derby's second oldest law firm is as strong as ever, and whilst retaining its air of history and continuity, changes in the law and new technology have made an enormous difference to the efficiency of the firm. The succeeding generations of Derby families who return again and again to the firm is testament to its long dedication to making their private and business lives run as smoothly and trouble-free as possible.

Top left: *Moody & Woolley's present day offices in St Mary's Gate.* ***Left:*** *Today's partners, Ian Griffiths and Julie Marson with the coveted Investors in People Award in January 2000.* ***Top right:*** *Opening of Probate House – the cutting of the ribbon was carried out by John Bather The Lord Lieutenant of Derbyshire in December 2004.* ***Below:*** *The 160th Anniversary Party held in the offices of Moody & Woolley at 40 St Mary's Gate in October 2006. The firm held a Costume Ball with the theme of the costumes taken from the three Centuries (19th, 20th and 21st) they have spanned.*

W W Winter - What a Picture!

The very much respected local photography firm W W Winter Ltd was established in the mid 1800s when photography was still in its infancy. William Walter Winter set up his business in 1864 on the north side of Midland Road before relocating across to the south side in 1867. The company's new studio was designed by the renowned Derby church architect Henry Isaac Stevens and had a row of church-like windows facing north along its length. These windows were needed to give as much diffused natural daylight lighting as possible because in those days there was no electricity and therefore photography relied totally upon daylight.

In the mid 1880s disaster struck when fire gutted the studio. Afterwards Winter re-organised the building and a new studio and artists' room were added. The building then contained about 30 rooms, including a number of galleries where paintings and porcelain were exhibited. There were specialised areas within the building where groups of workers concentrated on daylight contact printing and hand retouching of photographic prints. Winter's was also one of the first Derby companies to have central heating.

William Henry King joined the company in November 1896 as a photographic assistant, operator and retoucher. With his help, Winter's became one of the pioneers of flash photography which involved carefully igniting a magnesium-based powder which burnt away rapidly giving a brilliant burst of white light. As time went on, the portrait studio was eventually revolutionised by the installation of carbon-arc electric lighting equipment made by the electrical and mining engineers Davis of Derby, incidentally another long-established local company still in business today. Because at that time there was no municipal electricity supply, the power required for the studio arc lamps was produced by a generator on the premises and this made Winter's one of the first businesses in Derby to have electric lighting.

Winter's growing reputation for artistic photography and especially portraiture gradually spread and the company became a photographer to the royal family and in particular to King Edward VII. The firm often made trips to Chatsworth to photograph people there.

In 1904, Mr King became the general manager. In 1910 he formed a partnership with a Mr H B Sheppard and, together, they bought out Mr Winter, who then emigrated to Canada. Mr Sheppard sold his interest in the business to Mr King in 1930.

In 1947, Mr King's son, Austin, became managing director. Austin was succeeded by Mr W H King's grandson, Hubert King in 1975. Hubert, a member of the British Institute of Professional Photography for more 50 years, was given a Presidential Award in November 1986 for long and distinguished service to the Institute. As well as being the current managing director, Hubert is one of the company's principal portraitists.

Led by Hubert King, the present employees respect the company's time-honoured traditions of service and quality. Ever mindful of technical advances, the firm has kept pace with technology and now specialises in digital photography and advanced computerised image manipulation to give their customers the best photography available today, including sensitive restoration of old photographs. As Hubert King says, "Winter's now has the best of modern digital technology and techniques so that we can give our customers the high-quality photographic services they demand."

Above: William Walter Winter, founder of the company.
Below: Early 20th and 21st century pictures of the studio in Midland Road. Right: Two examples of modern portraits.

MHA - Love, Compassion and Respect

With a head office in Derby, MHA is a nationwide charity dedicated to improving the lives of older people. Based on the Christian principles of love, compassion and respect, for 65 years MHA has been providing high quality, person-centred care and support to older people throughout Britain, with a focus on nurturing spiritual and physical well-being. The charity offers residential, nursing and specialist dementia Care Homes, housing and support services.

The work is underpinned by the organisation's Christian values, professional standards and management, combined with the highest levels of care and support. All its services are founded on respect for individuality, personal choice and dignity.

MHA was founded by the Methodist Church in 1943 as an independent charity to provide care and support and accommodation for older people. In 1945 the charity's first Residential Care Home – Ryelands - was opened in Wallington, Surrey.

Further homes opened in quick succession throughout the 1940s and 1950s.

In 1977 MHA Housing services were established offering sheltered accommodation for rent. In 1988 MHA's 'Live at Home' initiative was set up providing befriending and social support to older people in their own homes, through volunteers.

The following year MHA's first Specialist Nursing Care Home was built.

In 1997 Specialist Dementia Care began to be delivered in purpose-built care homes, focussing on the person and their individual needs.

Housing with Care services was established in 2000, an initiative combining self-contained accommodation with 24 hour care and support by MHA staff on site. This was followed in 2004 by Community Services, set up to provide MHA's dementia care to people living in their own homes.

MHA benefits from the commitment of 4,000 staff, as well as the dedication of more than 5,000 volunteers in the delivery of care and support to 12,000 older people.

Today this Derby-based organisation is expanding to meet the needs and expectations of even more older people.

Inspired by Christian concern, MHA's strategy for the future is to continue to deliver a broad range of services, encompassing care homes, housing and community based services whilst continuing with its core mission: to improve the quality of life for older people.

Further information can be found by visiting the MHA website: www.mha.org.uk or by telephoning 01332 296200.

Pictures: *Staff providing high quality, person-centred care and support.*

Garrandale - Engineering Excellence

'From tiny acorns mighty oak trees grow'. And what is true of arboriculture is equally true of industrial enterprise. Derby and its environ contains many examples of local flair, enterprise and initiative which have created business which have become lasting monuments to the vision of their founders.

From starting up more than 30 years ago, in 1976, in a shed in a quarry (small business start up units did not exists then) the Garrandale Group has established itself a respected and versatile engineering company with a high quality portfolio of blue-chip customers in the engineering, automotive, rail, gas and oil industries.

From its small start, today the Garrandale Group has more than 100 skilled employees and an annual turnover of some six million pounds.

Garrandale specialises in 'one offs' and small batches. Recent products have included: Safety critical rail vehicle sub-frames, automated machines for MRI scanners and for 'Aviation' components ultrasonic inspection, transportation equipment for jet engines and military equipment, production of chassis for a range of co-ordinate measuring machines, repair and retrofitting of new equipment to rail vehicles, robotic assembly and welding machines for car bumpers, car seats and various other car components and fabrications in stainless steels, aluminium and mild steel.

Based in Alfreton Road, Derby, Garrandale has the benefit of a world-class engineering and manufacturing infrastructure on its doorstep.

The group has responded to the challenges of the leading technology companies of the 21st century, and with a skilled workforce supplied engineering solutions and quality products such as: Specialist high integrity welding and fabrication, safety critical rail vehicle components, production lines for rail vehicles, sophisticated body scanner production machines, and high speed automotive component assembly machines.

Today Garrandale offers comprehensive engineering services encompassing: Project management, design, electrical mechanical, manufacture, machining and fabrication, assembly, installation and site commissioning.

The firm is certified to ISO 9001-2000.

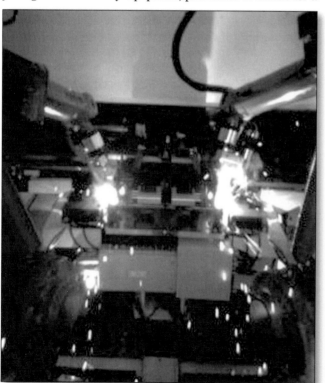

Top: Receiving the Derbyshire Business Awards in 1998. Left: A Garrandale welding robot. Below: Services provided by Garrandale: Special purpose machinery and tooling (top left), fabrication and machining (top right), installation and servicing (bottom left) and rail services (bottom right).

Picture The Past

In the past, anyone wanting to view the collections of hundreds of thousands of old images in the libraries and museums of Derbyshire or Nottinghamshire would have to travel many miles to try and track down the ones they were interested in. This proved to be frustrating and time consuming for researchers, a barrier to anyone from further a field as well as damaging to the more fragile images from all the handling. The collections include photographs, slides, negatives, glass plates, postcards and engravings recalling the history of our local communities for a hundred years and more.

Thankfully senior staff in four local authorities got their heads together to solve the problem and the idea of conserving the images using digitisation whilst at the same time giving people all over the world access to the digitised versions was conceived. Funding was obtained from the Heritage Lottery Fund at the beginning of 2002 together with additional cash from the four partner authorities, Derbyshire and Nottinghamshire County Councils and the City Councils of Derby and Nottingham. Local studies staff in the libraries and museums started collating images and information ready for inclusion in the project and sent out thousands of letters requesting copyright clearance from the original photographers or their relatives. Nick Tomlinson was appointed as project manager to lead a team of experienced professionals inputting the information into a custom-built database and carefully digitising the images.

The Picture the Past website (www.picturethepast.org.uk) was launched in June 2003 and by the end of 2006 in excess of 63,000 pictures had been added. It now attracts well over 10,000 visitors every month from all over the world viewing thousands of pages of images. The site is updated on a regular basis and actually gives the user the ability to 'correct' existing information or add more information to those pictures with scant details.

The website is designed to be as 'easy to use' as possible and includes a simple keyword search facility as well as more comprehensive search mechanisms for users looking for images with a particular theme or by a specific photographer. Visitors can print out low resolution copies for their own personal use or study purposes but for those users wanting to own a top quality glossy photographic copy the website includes an on-line ordering service. Thanks to the involvement of Derby Evening Telegraph this enables users to browse the collection and order and pay for their selections securely on-line. The prints are produced on state-of-the-art equipment and, as a non-profit making project, all the income raised from this service goes back into the conservation and preservation of more original pictures. This book gives you the chance to sample just a handful of the images contained in the website and it is very much hoped that you will go on to enjoy the rest of the pictures on the website.

For people who do not have access to the Internet at home, or who are not sure where to start, there are computers available for public use in all libraries and the local studies staff are more than willing to help you get started.

The website can be viewed at www.picturethepast.org.uk

Picture the Past

makes historic images

from the library & museum

collections of Derby,

Derbyshire, Nottingham

& Nottinghamshire,

freely available at the

click of a mouse button.

ACKNOWLEDGMENTS

The publishers would like to sincerely thank the following individuals and organisations
for their help and contribution to this publication

The Derby Evening Telegraph

W W Winter Photographers

Nick Tomlinson (www.picturethepast.org.uk)

Derby Museum and Art Gallery

Derby City Council

Andy Savage (www.derbyphotos.co.uk)

Dave Upton (www.daveuptonphotography.co.uk)

Mr C Sheppard

S Smith

Nigel Aspdin

R E Pearson

C B Sherwin

Frank Grimshaw